Parenting Across the Autism Spectrum

also by Ann Palmer

**Realizing the College Dream with Autism
or Asperger Syndrome**
A Parent's Guide to Student Success
ISBN 1 84310 801 1

of related interest

Asperger's Syndrome
A Guide for Parents and Professionals
Second Edition
Tony Attwood
ISBN 1 84310 307 9

Multicoloured Mayhem
Parenting the Many Shades of Adolescents
and Children with Autism, Asperger Syndrome and AD/HD
Jacqui Jackson
ISBN 1 84310 171 8

Homespun Remedies
Strategies in the Home and Community
for Children with Autism Spectrum and Other Disorders
Dion E. Betts and Nancy J. Patrick
ISBN 1 84310 813 5

How to Live with Autism and Asperger Syndrome
Practical Strategies for Parents and Professionals
Chris Williams and Barry Wright
Illustrated by Olive Young
ISBN 1 84310 184 X

Finding You Finding Me
Using Intensive Interaction to Get in Touch
with People whose Severe Learning Disabilities
are Combined with Autistic Spectrum Disorder
Phoebe Caldwell
ISBN 1 84310 399 0

Parenting Across the Autism Spectrum

Unexpected Lessons We Have Learned

Maureen F. Morrell and Ann Palmer

Jessica Kingsley Publishers
London and Philadelphia

First published in 2006
by Jessica Kingsley Publishers
116 Pentonville Road
London N1 9JB, UK
and
400 Market Street, Suite 400
Philadelphia, PA 19106, USA

www.jkp.com

Library of Congress Cataloging in Publication Data

Morrell, Maureen F.
  Parenting across the autism spectrum : unexpected lessons we have learned / Maureen F. Morrell
and Ann Palmer.
     p. cm.
  Includes bibliographical references.
  ISBN-13: 978-1-84310-807-8 (pbk.)
  ISBN-10: 1-84310-807-0 (pbk.)
  1. Autistic children--Popular works. 2. Autism in children--Popular works. I. Palmer, Ann. II.
Title.
  RJ506.A9M677 2006
  649'.154--dc22
                                                              2005037229

British Library Cataloguing in Publication Data
A CIP catalogue record for this book is available from the British Library

ISBN-13: 978 1 84310 807 8
ISBN-10: 1 84310 807 0

Printed and bound in the United States by Thomson-Shore, Inc.

*To my husband Rob – for bringing me tea
and talking me down from the ledge. To my sons Michael
and Patrick – for their steadfast support and unfailing
good humor. And to my son Justin – for being my heaviest
responsibility and my greatest gift.*
MFM

*I dedicate this book to my mother, Miriam Bly,
for her unwavering support and belief in me.*
AP

Contents

Acknowledgements

Over the years, Justin and Eric have been lucky to have many people who believed in them. We would especially like to thank Justin's and Eric's supportive peers: Johanna Wortham, David Prater, Christopher and Kathleen Dawson, Alex Matthews, Kyle Cory, Sarah and Philip Palmer, and Michael and Patrick Morrell; their wonderful teachers: Susie Gilbert, Karin Klieman, Kevin Greene, Nancy Stentz, Rex Best, Mitzi Safrit, Kim Banks, Barbara Davis, Jeanine Sellmer, Patricia Smith, Cathy Carr, Carla Nerison, and Deb Steinkopf; and their amazing care providers: Robin Speight, Tony Outlaw, Lester Outlaw, Chuck Lamothe, Kathy Byrne, Kim Czornij, and Jude Barrineau.

It has been our privilege to work with extraordinary consultants who taught us the meaning of "best practice": Lee Marcus, Pat Fennell, Nadine Waurin, Susan Robinson, Sharon Floyd, Joanne Medlin, Hal Shigley, Pam DiLavore, Christina Phillips, Mary Beth Rehm, Marie Bristol-Power, Laurie Eckenrode, Sue Buehner, and Mary Beth Van Bourgondien.

The advocacy efforts and personalized services of these autism organizations greatly improved the quality of life for Justin and Eric and for our families: Jill Hinton Keel and the staff of the Autism Society of North Carolina; Dawn Allen and the staff of GHA, Inc. and Carolina Farms; Nancy Reichle and the staff of the Carolina Living and Learning Center; and Lee Marcus and the staff of the Chapel Hill TEACCH Center.

We have been inspired, nurtured, encouraged, and thoroughly entertained by an amazing assortment of friends and family members in parenting our children with autism. We would especially like to thank the pioneer moms who opened the doors of opportunity for our children: Bobo Warren, Betty Camp, Jackie Ransdell, Marie Horne, and Joanne Jeffries; the members of the original Mothers' Group: Matty Chadderton, Becky Angel, Toni Small, Mary Boykin, Thea Gardner, Chris Reagan, Susan Monk, Beth Grunewald, Sherry Anscher, Marianne Rosenman, Alice Wertheimer, and Starla Gilpin; and our loyal cheering section: Clare Casale, Carol Offen, Diane Hartill, Regan McCarthy, Pat Donohue, Chuck Lamothe, Deb Dawson, Stan Yancey,

Jim and Mary Ragsdale, Kathy O'Brien, Elizabeth Ross, Kate Hall, Fran Muller, Marty Kellogg, Sandy Reiser, Joanne Evans, Mark and Jan Pfeifer, Jan Carroll, Hal and Kathy Baumann, Kathy McMackin, Susie King, Kat Moncol, and members of the FitzGerald, Morrell, Palmer, and Bly families.

We are grateful for the constant supply of support, critique, and enthusiasm from the people who helped us complete this book. We especially want to thank Nancy Huber for opening the door, and Darla Coffey for helping us walk through; Bobby Palmer, Rob Morrell, and Kathy Baumann for their invaluable editing advice; Terri Meyers, Linda Griffin, Dave Spicer, and Emily Ballance for their insight and stories; and Marty Kellogg, Chris Reagan, and Thea Gardner for giving us suggestions (and gourmet meals) while we worked on this book.

Introduction

When Eric and Justin were first diagnosed, we knew that life as we had planned it was over. This new life after autism felt grim and sad, and the future looked bleaker still. Yet two decades later that future is now, and it is neither grim nor bleak. The grief that can still overwhelm us no longer comes from our children's arrival in our lives, but from their departure as young men for their new lives. How did the future turn out to be so different from the one we had imagined?

We met at a mothers' support group at the University of North Carolina – Chapel Hill in 1986. Still reeling from the diagnoses of our children, we came searching for help and for hope. As each mother described her child, our autism stereotypes started to fade. Though sharing the same diagnosis, each child had a unique combination of deficits and strengths. Eric and Justin were on opposite ends of the autism spectrum. Eric was a quiet and passive child, who entertained himself easily. His disruptive behaviors were infrequent and resulted from changes in his routine. Although his intelligence tested in the normal range, his language delays and social impairments made it difficult for him to communicate his needs. Justin, on the other hand, was a whirlwind of activity, a child who required constant one-to-one supervision. His moods changed constantly, shifting from affectionate and content to self-injurious and aggressive (and everywhere in between). He had significant limitations in all areas of development.

Yet such differences in our children never mattered much in the mothers' group. As the generation of mothers who came before the current autism "epidemic," we were too few in number to subdivide into factions. We knew that our children's functioning levels influenced their need for services, especially in school. We recognized that some parenting issues were different: Ann did not contend with Justin's self-care needs, and Maureen did not have to deal with Eric's self--awareness of his condition. Yet we soon discovered that the parenting experience, the worries, confusion, and grief, were more similar than different. We recognized in each other's eyes what had brought us to the threshold of the mothers' group: the "deer in the headlights" fear of parenting a child with autism.

Dr. Lee Marcus, a skilled psychologist, created a safe haven for us to examine the new realities of our lives. Here we could share our fears and frustrations and, eventually, our solutions and triumphs. Throughout the years we cried (often), complained (even more often), laughed (eventually), and learned (more than we ever imagined). And the way we grew was by finding ourselves in each other's story.

Listening to the stories of the mothers' group was like coming home, like finding a place of kindred spirits. We were no longer alone in our attempts to cope with this life after autism. We could shed the tremendous sense of isolation that compounded our grief. For it was grief that we felt – not in the neat, linear stages described by researchers, but as a confusing combination of frightening and dark emotions that were hard to describe. Hearing others' descriptions helped us identify and name our own confusing feelings, reducing them to a size we could handle. Hearing someone else tell her story helped us to better understand our own. This self-awareness produced the clarity and perspective that helped us regain some control over our lives. The stories sometimes were troubling to hear and to tell. But the courage of mothers honestly sharing their struggles and challenges inspired each of us to be more courageous. Each mother was also grateful that her child did not have *all* the autism symptoms described in those sessions. For the symptoms our children did have, these stories provided practical information. The advice from the mothers of older children was especially helpful since they had the experience of "field-testing" the advice proffered by the professionals. Those parents helped us learn how to manage our day-to-day lives, providing the "how-to" tips on living with a child with autism. Their perspective and sense of proportion helped us regain our lost sense of humor. They prepared us for what would come next. Most important of all, they restored our hope that if other mothers could "survive and advance," so could we.

This book describes how we have survived and advanced to a future so different from the one we had imagined or feared. Here are the experiences, lessons, and surprising consolations we have found in parenting two very different children with autism, children on opposite ends of the spectrum. This book presents what we know now, as our adult children leave home, that we wish we had known when they were first diagnosed. It offers the opportunity to listen in on a conversation between the mothers we were then and the mothers we are today. We recognize that there have been rapid and dramatic changes in the autism landscape since Eric and Justin were first diagnosed. In the 1980s the incidence of autism was 1 in 5000 births and the public was largely unaware of what the diagnosis entailed. When we introduced our children as "autistic," people often congratulated us for having an "artistic" child. By 2005, the incidence of autism has made the almost incomprehensible leap to nearly 1 in 166 births (Centers for Disease Control and Prevention, National Center on Birth Defects and Developmental Disabilities 2005). Now there are virtually no degrees of separation between autism and the general public.

Yet it is also true that the more things change, the more they stay the same. The four core realities that confronted us as new mothers in 1980 still confront new mothers today. There is no consensus on what causes autism. There is continuing controversy over whether autism can or should be cured. There is no widely shared opinion on which education and treatment approach is most effective. And the decision on what course of action to take still rests with overwhelmed parents. There is a saying that "If you have met one child with autism, you have met one child with autism." The same uniqueness applies to each parent. Ultimately, every parent must find his or her own way. Our stories and lessons are meant to be a companion on the journey, making it a bit easier and a little less lonely.

Our book is intended for the worried parents of children with autism, for the people who care about them, and for the professionals who want to help them. This book is not meant to be a prescription for successful parenting. There are already too many voices in the autism world claiming the corner on truth and right. If we have learned anything over the years, it is to be wary of people who proclaim they have all the answers! But while the only shoes we have walked in are our own, parents of children with autism tread many of the same paths. To borrow a theme from 12-step programs, we hope to share with parents and professionals the experience, strength, and hope we have found in ourselves, our families, our friends, and the other parents we have mentored over the last 20 years. We will do this by telling our stories.

There can be disadvantages in writing a retrospective account of living with autism. Time and distance may diminish the intensity of the experience, softening the edges of the grief and pain that we felt. There can be a tendency to put a "glass is half full" spin on past events that at the time made us want to shatter that bone-dry glass against the nearest wall. Yet as Kierkegaard said, "Life is lived forward but understood backward" (Kierkegaard 1948, p.102). With empty-nest time to reflect on our experiences, it is only now that we see the growth and changes in our children and in ourselves that were hidden to us in the demanding present of those early days. These more recent insights embolden us to offer this account of what we have lost and gained, the lessons learned, and the surprising consolations found in parenting Eric and Justin.

Chapter 1

Rebuilding Life after Autism
Ann's Story

It was a phone call in 1985 that started my life down this different path. My son Eric was two years old at the time and the call was from his pre-school teacher. She was concerned that Eric might have a hearing problem. He wasn't responding when she called his name and he seemed oblivious to the other kids in the class. The call totally surprised me because I had no idea Eric was having any problems in preschool. I felt sure his hearing was fine, but I respected the teacher's concerns and scheduled a speech and hearing evaluation for Eric.

While waiting for the date of the appointment I studied Eric and tried to remember anything he might have done that was different, that was not within the norm. He had always been a perfect baby. He rarely cried. He slept well. He ate well. As a first-time mom I had consulted the baby books (probably too often!) and Eric had reached all the developmental milestones on time. He was even doing some things ahead of schedule, such as knowing all his ABCs (upper and lower case) by the age of one and a half. His granddad had made him a beautiful set of wooden letter blocks and Eric loved bringing us letters, telling us what the letter was and then saying the name of something that started with that letter. How could anything be wrong with a child who could be so bright and so adorable? I convinced myself that he was fine.

On the day of the evaluation, the speech clinician sat down with me to go over the results. I really don't remember much of what she said that day. The only thing I remember clearly was her asking me if I had ever heard of autism. I studied psychology in college and I definitely remembered autism. The picture that came to my mind was of a child sitting in a corner, rocking, in his own little world. Even though I knew that picture did not describe my son, I found myself crying while she spoke to me that day. At some level I must have known it was possible that what she was saying was true.

Denial is a funny thing. I understand its purpose to protect us from the pain that our minds or hearts can't handle. When the speech clinician mentioned possible autism, I could not see the autism in my son. I could find a logical reason for everything that was different about Eric. I went to the public library and looked at what few books there were about autism and none of the case studies I could find described a child like mine. Our friends and family members also couldn't believe it could be autism. Everyone had a story of someone they knew who didn't do this by then, or did something weird as a child but eventually grew out of it. I took Eric to our pediatrician and told him about the speech clinician's concerns. After just a few minutes with us in the examining room the pediatrician said to me, "Look at him. He's talking. He can't be autistic. If he is autistic, then I'm the Pope!" This was a professional, a trusted, knowledgeable member of the medical community. How could he be wrong?

We eventually took Eric to a developmental pediatrician who had many years' experience with children with autism. Eric was almost three years old when this pediatrician officially gave us the diagnosis. We met in her beautiful home where she made Eric and my husband and me feel very relaxed and comfortable. She spent several hours with Eric, examining him physically, observing him playing, and watching how he interacted with us. She also asked us many questions about Eric's early development and how he was at home, at school, and with other children. It was a long and thorough evaluation and we felt confident that she was considering all the information possible to make her determination. It was very different from my earlier experience at the other pediatrician's office when the doctor dismissed my concerns so quickly. Although the news was not good and hearing about Eric's autism changed our lives forever, I will always remember the kindness and sensitivity this pediatrician showed us that day in her home.

I remember a physical pain. It's hard to describe but I felt it deep inside of me. I cried for several days, performing all the necessary tasks such as taking care of my children, eating, bathing, etc., but I walked around like a zombie. I isolated myself that first week and stayed at home and cried and avoided the people who meant the most to me.

They wanted to help me but if I saw them or spoke to them it was too hard to keep up the protective wall I had built around myself. I hated being so vulnerable. My husband was grieving too, but doing it alone. He didn't want to add to my pain by letting me see the pain he was in. I knew he was hurting, but emotionally and physically I didn't have anything left to be able to comfort him.

There was also a feeling of everything being out of control. This "thing" had invaded our lives and taken over. I couldn't make it go away. I couldn't even understand it. My beautiful little boy had not changed, but in reality everything had changed. The way I looked at him and talked to him changed. The way I thought about myself had changed. My life, Eric's life, and my family's life had changed and I had no control over it. I wanted to be able to control my emotions and stop crying, but I couldn't even do that.

I thought this emotional and physical pain would last forever, but it didn't. I don't know how long it took and I don't know exactly why things changed, but at a certain point I stopped crying all day and started to take control of my life again. My husband and I found a way to comfort each other and to be strong together. I was able to open up again to the people who cared about me and to allow them to help me. I stopped crying and started learning how to help my child.

The first couple of years following the diagnosis were especially hard. At the time of Eric's diagnosis our daughter was six weeks old and sleep was a luxury. My husband was in a very stressful job and I was barely functioning. Eric was still the beautiful and smart little boy we treasured, but I found myself analyzing everything he did. Why is he doing that? Is that part of the autism? Is he getting worse? It was very hard to relax and enjoy him. I threw myself into his therapy. I worked with him daily at home, drove him to private speech and occupational therapy, and took him to two preschools: one "typical" preschool and a speech and language preschool. We also went to weekly sessions at Division TEACCH (Treatment and Education of Autistic and related Communication handicapped CHildren). All of these therapies and schools helped him immensely but I was exhausted and felt like I was living in my car. In retrospect, as hard as it was, I know now that I needed to be that involved with his therapy. I needed to read everything I could get my hands on. That was *my* therapy, my way of coping. It helped me feel more in control of my life at a time when everything felt very "out of control."

I don't think I could have survived without the support of my husband and my family and the support I received from other mothers of autistic children whom I met. I became involved in a mothers' support group at TEACCH. It was a unique collection of mothers from all walks of life with many different experiences and backgrounds. The children we represented were mostly boys, of various ages, and all over the spectrum of autism. Some had mental retardation and some did not. Some were included or mainstreamed in regular education classes, and some were in self-contained autism or special education classes.

Despite all of our differences, we mothers had many similarities. We all were overwhelmed and exhausted from too little sleep and too many therapies and interventions. We had the "deer in the headlights" look as we sat around the table, waiting for the next thing to leap out of the dark and hit us. We all felt guilty about something: guilty about not doing enough or doing too much, guilty about waiting too long or starting too early, guilty about the choices we made and the ones we didn't make.

We came together at a unique time. We followed those brave parents who battled the world's misconceptions about the causes of autism and fought for the rights of individuals with autism. We came before the current "epidemic" of autism and the bombardment of information, therapies, and "cures" that are so frequent in the media today. We were the pre-internet, pre-*Rainman* generation of mothers, searching for information and reasons for why we were there. We needed each other, and the close friendships we developed then remain with us today.

It was important for me to have the support of other parents at a time when Eric's behaviors were becoming more and more difficult. Eric was very rigid in his routines and would have horrible meltdowns when something changed or unpredictable things happened. He would sometimes cry uncontrollably for hours. Nothing I could do would console him. He would get upset if I drove a different route to the grocery store or if the video rental store was out of his favorite video. He would get upset if one of the foods on his plate touched another food. You would think the world was coming to an end if he missed the beginning of a favorite television show. It was hardest when I had no idea why he was upset. From Eric's point of view, something wasn't happening as it should have and I often didn't know what it was or how to fix it. In order to avoid the stress of these difficult behaviors, our family lost all spontaneity. Before we did anything or went anywhere we had to ask ourselves how Eric would react. New situations were avoided if at all possible, and, because outings into the community could be so difficult, we found ourselves staying home more and more.

During these early years it felt as though time was standing still and I would never see the other side. In reality, the whirlwind, difficult early days gradually slowed down and life became more manageable. I began to understand Eric's autism and how to help him. As Eric's language improved, his ability to tell us when something was wrong or tell us what he wanted also improved. He began to understand more of what we were saying to him and we could forewarn him about what would be coming next. Before his language skills improved he was frustrated and confused by the world around him. When he began to feel less out of control in his world and as he was better able to understand others and express himself, the meltdowns decreased and gradually disappeared.

A different chapter began in our lives when Eric entered public school. There was a whole new world I needed to learn about. There were countless people to talk to, new acronyms to learn, and a big system to navigate. I had to learn about Eric's and my rights and how to connect with people who would be providing services and support to my son. I was worried about special education. I remember crying the day Eric was first diagnosed when I thought about him in a "special ed" class. I pictured him in a class like the special education classes in the schools I attended growing up. The students in those classes were separated as much as possible from the "normal" kids. Everyone knew who they were but no one spoke to them. I was scared for Eric to be in a class like that.

I was wrong to fear special education and I learned very quickly that the services and support available for exceptional students were much better than I had imagined. Eric's first years in public school were in a self-contained autism class with five students and a well-trained teacher and aide. Although the students were all different and had varying challenges and strengths, they were all considered high-functioning. This particular class filled a need for these students who did not quite fit into the typical autism classes but still were not ready to be in regular education classes.

These were years of incredible progress for Eric and two of the most relaxing years for me as his mother. I didn't feel as though I always had to be on alert to fight for Eric or to protect him. The teachers understood his autism, cared for him, and made sure he was challenged and safe. They set up mainstream opportunities for Eric in the regular education classes, gradually increasing the time out of the autism class as he developed the skills he needed. The autism class teacher would choose the regular education teachers who wanted these students and were willing to work with them. It was a win–win situation. I didn't know how good a situation we had until we lost it.

In retrospect, I understand now how helpful those years in a self-contained setting were to Eric's future success in regular education classes. Many parents of children with Asperger Syndrome or high-functioning autism may feel that their child's being in a special education setting somehow diminishes the chances of a good prognosis for the future. They may connect success in school to full inclusion in the regular education classes. A smaller class size with more one-to-one attention can be a good start for the student on the spectrum who may struggle with sensory or social issues. It is important to look at each individual child, what he or she can handle, and consider whether a smaller classroom setting with a good teacher could be an appropriate option. Being placed in a self-contained special education class does not necessarily mean the child will always be in that type of setting.

After Eric's two years in the autism class, the school system decided not to offer the class any longer. Eric was placed in a regular third-grade class, fully included without any special accommodations and without an aide. It was difficult for Eric to be in a large class with so many students all day. The noise level and constant activity and movement around the class were a big adjustment for him. It was easy for him to get "lost in the shuffle" because he didn't ask for help if he needed it. He was so withdrawn and quiet that he rarely attracted the teacher's attention. This transition to third grade was one of Eric's hardest years and the first of ten years that he spent fully included in regular education classes. We found some years to be better than others. Some teachers were more supportive than others and some years Eric struggled more academically. But overall Eric was successful in the inclusive setting. He was successful because he was quiet, followed all the rules, and did fairly well with the academics. He didn't require a lot of extra work and most teachers found it rewarding to have him in their classes.

Advocating for Eric in an inclusion setting was very different from what I had experienced in the autism class setting. I had to be much more involved at the school, and offered to support the teachers any way I could. That included sharing information about autism and about Eric, or volunteering in the classes and on field trips. The regular education teachers often knew very little about the autism spectrum and were sometimes nervous about having a child with autism in the class. I frequently had to convince them that having Eric in their class would not be too difficult. My advocating also involved continually defending Eric's need for supports and services. Over the years there were times when Eric was doing well academically and the school would suggest removing his autism label. They did not realize that without the organizational and visual strategies Eric was receiving, he would not be as successful.

As Eric got older I started to worry more and more about his upcoming adolescence. I had heard horror stories of children with autism developing seizure disorders and severe behavior issues during adolescence. I knew "typical" adolescence was difficult for parents to survive, so I figured adolescence with autism must be unbearable. I worried for years, waiting for this dreaded stage of our lives that fortunately never really came. Eric reached his teenage years and, except for the physical changes, he barely changed at all. His personality remained fairly easygoing and quiet and no new behaviors started. Of course the kids around him changed, and finding peers who were willing to accept or help Eric became more difficult. The middle-school years were actually the hardest but we survived them. In fact, the middle-school and high-school years were a time of great learning and maturity for Eric.

Time has changed so many things. When I look at our lives now and remember my fears of the future when Eric was first diagnosed, I am amazed by how much he has changed and what he has accomplished. I could not have imagined how far Eric would come and how far I would come as his mother. The autism I didn't understand or accept is now such a part of our daily lives that we sometimes don't even think about it. Our family feels very normal most of the time. Eric is 22 and a wonderful young man. He has accomplished so much and we are very proud of him. He is a student at a large state university where he is studying anthropology and zoology. (That animal obsession is finally being put to good use!) He lives on campus in a dormitory and comes home for visits every other weekend. His autism is still a big part of who he is and always will be. He continues to "stim" quite a bit, pacing and talking to himself sometimes, and he still isn't very social and usually prefers to be alone. He is a man of few words, answering questions when asked but not initiating many conversations. His rigidity as a child has improved, and he's much more flexible and handles change well. There are no more behavior problems or "meltdowns," thank goodness.

Parents of newly diagnosed children, who are in the middle of that overwhelming, scary time of adjustment, need to hear that it will get better. Our children are always learning and will develop in ways that we may not expect. Dealing with the really difficult times gets easier, not necessarily because the situations are easier, but because with time we as parents become stronger. The experiences we live through and the things we learn from our children over the years give us more confidence in our abilities to make the right decisions. We continue to have situations that scare and overwhelm us and we may always fear for our children's futures. But there are always strategies to try, people to go to and to lean on, and lessons to be learned. In the following chapters Maureen and I will be sharing some of the things we have learned about ourselves, our children, and about autism. We hope that our experiences will help you to feel that you are not alone and that there *is* life after autism. For lessons in rebuilding life after autism, see the box at the end of Chapter 2.

Chapter 2

Rebuilding Life after Autism
Maureen's Story

Justin's test results read like a telegram: *Profound Mental Retardation.* STOP. *Chromosome Abnormality.* STOP. *Severe Autism.* STOP. The professionals explained the reports, but those were the only words I could hear. Later I would understand that the lack of oxygen from the double-wrapped umbilical cord at Justin's traumatic birth was not the primary cause of his developmental delays. That was just a little bonus. Some spontaneous mutation of his cells had occurred before I knew I was pregnant, leaving an extra piece of Chromosome #15 and permanent flaws in the developmental blueprint of his brain. I had to admit that my special educator husband had been right all along. He had recognized the severity of Justin's problems from the moment of his birth. Clinging to my glass-is-half-full worldview, I had minimized Justin's developmental delays, despite my own training as a pediatric nurse.

As we left the Developmental Evaluation Center that day in 1981, Rob tried to console me by pointing out that at least now we knew the real source of Justin's problems. For a moment I felt the relief that comes with a definitive diagnosis. Then a new realization began to set in. The three-year-long battle I had been waging between despair and hope was over. Despair had won.

With the confirmation of our worst fears, I felt lost and inconsolably sad. I had expected a child with unlimited potential, a Justin who would be the perfect combination of all of our best qualities. It is the dream that all parents share. We believe our children hold the potential to be the best at everything they do. Being new parents, we fail to see that their lives will be more like the television commercial where a beautiful, curly-haired little girl sits serenely eating a bowl of cereal. While she

.   23 eats, the narrator recites the long list of fabulous accomplishments that lie in store for this little girl. As we ponder whether she will become a star athlete, an accomplished scholar, or a future President of the United States, she calmly picks up the bowl of cereal and dumps it over her head. Eventually, all our children will calmly dump their bowls of cereal over their heads. But by the time we recognize their imperfections, we are so caught up in the fascinating reality of who they really are, perfection no longer matters. Our dreams of their perfection gradually disappear over time. This newly diagnosed Justin was so different from the child I had expected that my dreams imploded immediately. I felt abandoned to care for an impostor.

Living with this impostor turned my dreams of the perfect family into a nightmare. From a passive and undemanding infant, Justin turned into a possessed version of the Energizer Bunny. A tornado of constant activity, Justin left a trail of destruction (his) and confusion (ours) in his wake. Unpredictability defined his moods, as he swung from a happy, affectionate child to a self-injurious, aggressive one in warp speed. Justin reacted to everything around him – everything except our attempts to calm, contain, or console him. His cluelessness in relating to the world was exceeded only by our parental cluelessness in relating to him. In my dreams of Justin as the perfect child, he was accompanied by the perfect mother. I planned to be that all-wise and all-loving perfect mom, a close approximation of Mother Teresa had she chosen the biological route. Justin the impostor, however, was not so lucky. Instead, he inherited a mom who felt torn by the best and the worst of her maternal connections.

I had experienced the ferocious attachment of motherhood when Justin went into the intensive care unit right after birth. While the umbilical cord may have been cut at delivery, I had a visceral understanding that the emotional umbilical cord would be there for life. I was shocked at the strength of that bond; such a powerful connection with a child I'd known for less than a day! It was my initiation into the "momma bear" mode of motherhood: that strong, instantaneous, and potentially deadly response to any threat to one of her "cubs." (There is also a "poppa bear" response, which can be equally strong and scary.) All parents experience this heightened state of readiness that prepares us to protect and defend our children when we perceive danger. However, the response becomes super-sized for parents of children with autism because life can feel so full of threats. We are always preparing for when, not if, the next crisis will arise.

If I was surprised at the power of my maternal attachment to Justin, I was shocked at the equally unmaternal feelings I tried to ignore. His desperate unhappiness felt like a reproach to my maternal efforts to console him. When I was honest with myself, I resented him for being so difficult. I blamed him for robbing me of a future that held any chance for happiness. I believed he had ruined my life. It would take me many years to admit that, in my dreams and fantasies, I wished he had never been born. Even now, those emotions make me shudder.

In retrospect, I understand that my ambivalence was a particularly difficult struggle, because I was forced to confront wounds from my past. In my attempt to redeem the less-than-perfect parts of my own childhood, I had spent a lifetime building my self-worth around the image of myself as the ultimate caregiver. Now I realized that I was not only capable of loving my child, I was capable of hating him as well. I was horrified at the mother I had become.

The luxury of time allows me to reflect on those early experiences with Justin. As a young parent, however, it took all my time and energy just to make it through the day. Researchers often describe grief as a progression from one stage to the next, moving to a final stage of acceptance. My experience of grief was much less orderly. I felt like an all-news radio station: all emotion, all the time. Overwhelmed by the enormity of Justin's needs, I alternated between paralysis and hyperactivity.

Fear was the most difficult emotional companion in my early life with Justin. I felt haunted by an endless cycle of unanswerable questions, especially at night. Would we be able to provide for Justin and his many needs? Would our marriage make it through the struggles and challenges of this difficult child? Did we have the capacity as individuals and as a couple to love him when he could act so unlovable? Would it be fair or even humanly possible to raise other children in this environment?

If life was this difficult at home, how would we manage the world outside our door? If we did not understand Justin's behavior, how would other people react? How would we keep him safe and protected when he was so reckless and vulnerable? Some mornings I found him shivering in bed, having kicked off his covers during the night. His inability even to cover himself with a blanket when he was cold made me question his potential to survive the more complicated problems that life would present. Given his significant problems with self-injury and aggression, I obsessed about what would happen when Justin grew bigger and stronger than I was. I catastrophized that if we were barely managing his behavior now, he was in danger of living his future life in the stereotypical back ward of some state institution.

Fear intensified my need to "fix" Justin and fueled my efforts to work with him all the time. I held a distorted belief that if he did not learn everything by the age of five, his life after five would be purely custodial. I worried if Justin did not learn to talk, he would never be able to communicate his needs. Feeling totally inadequate, yet desperately in charge, I ran from one therapist to the next, trying all the different approaches then in vogue. None of them offered the quick fix that I sought.

Consumed by my obsession with Justin's deficits, I missed the initial signs when life began to improve. This gradual shift, from life as a blur to life with some focus, reminds me of the infamous transition phase of pregnancy. Convinced that you have reached the time in your labor when you are ready to die, you actually are ready to deliver. Moving through that stage of transition changes everything.

At first, life was better because of what was *not* happening – sleep was not being interrupted, Justin was not having tantrums in public and I was not having meltdowns in private. After living in a world of negatives, we somehow got back to zero. Then as evidence of Justin's slow but real capacity for growth became obvious, we began to experience a world with some positives. His functional skills started to emerge. Some of the skills he acquired resulted from many "opportunities" to practice. For example, from kicking his shoes off every hour of every day, Justin mastered the art and science of putting his shoes *on*.

Other skills emerged with their own sense of timing. We had tried unsuccessfully to help Justin replace his tantrums with more effective ways to communicate what he wanted. Then, one day at school, he had a communication epiphany. His excited teacher called to tell us that Justin had taken her by the hand, and, leading her outside the classroom and down the hall, had placed her hand firmly on the handle of a wagon. Making eye contact that spoke volumes, he seemed to say, "Enough already with the desk work. I am ready to ride." From then on, his days were filled with wagon-ride opportunities to practice his newly discovered understanding of cause and effect.

As his functional and nonverbal communication skills increased, Justin's behavior became more predictable. He used facial and verbal cues to signal an impending meltdown, allowing us to restructure the environment. He showed us that taking a "power walk" could often help calm him down. During his teenage years, Justin developed his most important behavior management skill: he learned to give himself a "time-out" by leaving a situation before he fell apart.

It seemed that Justin was finally beginning to understand parts of his world. He could get his brain synapses firing in ways that helped him to focus and solve problems. As his skills and his understanding increased, I believe he found the world a less frightening place.

As a mother, I have experienced the truth of the saying that "you are only as happy as your least happy child." As Justin showed more enjoyment in life, I found more enjoyment in being his mom. As he learned new skills to manage the world, so did I. My search for definitive answers has never been as successful as I'd hoped. My black-and-white worldview struggled with all of autism's grays. But in my search to find people to help us, I found reason for hope and much more.

I found a generation of parents whose pioneering efforts pried open the doors of opportunity for Justin, doors that had been closed to their own sons and daughters. I found many professionals – underpaid, overworked and undervalued – who treated me as a partner in teaching Justin, even when effective approaches proved hard to find. I found friends and family whose presence told me that they might not know where I was going, but that I did not have to go there alone. I found "autism moms" who *did* know this journey, and they offered me a lifeline with their own stories, their hope and their strength.

From listening to other mothers and subsequently becoming a mother of what our friend Matty calls my two "severely normal" children, I learned that we all grow into this motherhood role over time. To be a mother is to face fear, uncertainty, insecurity, sadness, and even ambivalence. For evidence of maternal ambivalence, we need only examine our fairy tales, cartoons, and nursery rhymes. (For example, what do we really mean when we sing "When the bough breaks, the cradle will fall"?) In one of my favorite *New Yorker* cartoons, two parent goldfish are swimming with a school of their offspring. One parent says to the other, "I guess we would be considered a family. We're living together. We love each other. And we haven't eaten the children yet."

Becoming a mother to a child with autism is an intense and exaggerated form of motherhood. None of us is prepared for the job. Recovering from grief is a most inexact science. In the early days, we all spin our wheels, searching for traction. For me the confluence of time, experience, and support helped me move on with my life.

Time is probably the truest, yet least satisfactory, answer to why life gets better. It challenges our carefully guarded illusion that we are in control of our lives. Time allows the brain's hard wiring for biological and psychological adaptation to work its hidden magic. Over time, our hearts and our psyches possess more powers of regeneration than we know. Ultimately, in the words of Anne Lamott, "time and showing up turn most messes to compost, and something surprising may grow..." (Lamott 2005, p.76).

With time, I gained experience. Each crisis I survived helped build my parental confidence that I would land on my feet the next time. As a lifelong catastrophizer, I would approach situations wondering what was the worst that could happen. This, I have learned, is *not* a good question to pose to oneself as a parent of a child with autism. Yet living to tell the tale of how I survived the latest unexpected autism challenge made me less fearful of the future. Eleanor Roosevelt wrote, "You gain strength, courage, and confidence by every experience in which you really stop to look fear in the face. You must do the things you think you can't do" (Roosevelt 1960, p.29). By doing the things we think we can't do, we learn to survive and advance.

Somewhere along the line, life stopped feeling like a tragedy and just became what it was. Living with unpredictability became the only predictable pattern of our lives. Balance and humor returned; regrets and comparisons faded. It is difficult to remember when this transition occurred, but I did find this entry in my journal: "Justin is six today. I can't believe that we have survived for six years. More than survived – we have a relatively normal, happy life. At least more normal than I had expected. During these six years, the pain has always overshadowed the pleasure. It amazes me that, on many days, the pleasure of having Justin in my life now outweighs the pain."

It's not that living with Justin became easy – it did not. It's not that pain and sadness did not recur – they did (and still do). But as Justin began to learn and mature, he developed some mastery over his life. And as I began to learn and mature, I developed some mastery over mine. Although our progress could be excruciatingly slow and our resistance to change legendary, Justin and I (along with his dad and his brothers) forged a life together as a family. Grief had blinded us to Justin's courage and spirit. Our vision gradually cleared as we grew in love. No longer an impostor, Justin became for us who he is and no longer who he was not.

Today, Justin is 27 years old. He lived at home with our family until two years ago, and now lives in a residential farm community designed for people with autism. Despite the severity of his autism and mental retardation, his functional, communication, and behavioral skills gained momentum in his young adult years and have continued to grow. While he has never developed the ability to talk, even the untrained observer would testify that Justin can communicate his needs. He developed strengths in gross motor activities; his lifting, moving, and carrying come in handy for work on the farm. He has also become the king of the "put-ins," which translates into jobs like putting soil into the garden pots, putting seeds in the soil in the garden pots, and putting water on the seeds in the soil in the garden pots. (Do you think I've spent enough time organizing task sequences?)

In discussing Justin's work on the farm, I do not want to leave the impression that he has become a hard worker. A strong work ethic has never been his "peak skill;" left on his own, he would be a real slug. While his ability to focus on tasks has improved, his real interests and skills are recreational. He would much rather smile engagingly at you while placing your hand on his back for a massage, or joining in activities like skating, hiking, eating, and riding in the car.

When he comes home for a visit, Justin also loves to hang out in his room, where we sometimes engage in a tug of war with his blanket. From that time long ago when the purpose of a blanket eluded his understanding, he now clings to his blanket to hide from the necessity of getting out of bed. His difficult behaviors have lessened, though at times he still struggles with self-injury and aggression. But he is no longer the extremely high-maintenance child of his youth. Rob jokes that we should have placed him in the group home as a child, then taken him back as he entered these easier-going adult years.

Lessons for rebuilding life after autism

Looking back, Ann and I recognize that the early days after the autism diagnosis were the hardest. Our friends who are "autism moms" would agree. We found that our anxieties about what would happen in the future were much worse than the realities we eventually faced. If the moms of adults that we are today could give any advice to the scared, grieving moms we were over two decades ago, this is what we would say:

1. Take a deep cleansing breath. Take another. And another. And another...

2. Despite all present evidence to the contrary, you will not always feel this sad, anxious, and fearful.

3. No one is endowed with the superhuman ability to be the perfect parent.

4. You will grow into the role of parent. With each crisis you survive, you will become less fearful of the future.

5. By the time you face the problems you fear in the future, you will be a different parent – more experienced, more confident, and more knowledgeable.

6. Life will remain unpredictable, but you will adjust.

7. Life will be hard, but not all the time.

8. There is no one right way to help your child with autism. You and your child will find your own way.

9. Resist the impulse to live in the future. Concentrate on living for – and improving – today.

10. Take it one day at a time (sometimes one hour at a time).

11. Autism will not always define your life. It recedes as time passes, becoming a part of your life but no longer your whole focus.

12. You will find consolations in this experience that you never expected to find.

Chapter 3

Balancing Family Life
The Siblings

Juggling the demands of family life is a balancing act for all families. Parents work to meet the emotional needs of each family member while stretching time, energy, and finances to cover the ever-increasing activities of daily living. Adding a child with autism to the family intensifies and complicates this balancing act. We make constant adjustments as we weigh the requirements for one child against the needs of the family as a whole.

Maureen

Rob left special education and entered medical school when Justin was eight months old. Michael was born just before medical school graduation and Patrick arrived to complete the "My Three Sons" theme of our family at the end of Rob's medical residency. Upon completing the residency program, the job-hunting process revealed the balancing act our family life had become.

Rob was offered several positions in four different states. I accompanied him on visits to explore potential neighborhoods and investigate regular and special education programs. Each day, I tried to decide what move would be best for our family. Each day, the criteria for making that decision changed.

On day one, I decided we needed to do what was best for Rob. After all, the journey from his return to college for a B.S. degree to the end of his medical training had taken nine years of hard work and sacrifice. He deserved to choose the job that he wanted.

On day two, I decided we needed to do what was best for Justin. After all, he was the most vulnerable member of our family. He deserved the best services available with all the supports that would help him develop his full potential.

On day three, I decided we needed to do what was best for Michael and Patrick. After all, they had already given up a large share of parental attention as they accommodated Rob's grueling schedule and Justin's need for my close supervision. They deserved to be put at the top of the list for a change.

On day four, I decided that we needed to do what was best for me. After all, I was the glue that held the family together. I deserved to live where I would be happy. Besides, my family lived by the maxim, "If Mama ain't happy, ain't nobody happy."

In the end, our move represented a compromise. Not the best move for any one family member, but a move to a job and community that was good enough for each one of us. As a close friend once laughingly told me, "If everyone in the family feels just a little bit screwed, you probably got the balance just about right."

Parents worry how autism will test the health and resilience of family relationships. In this chapter and Chapter 4 we have focused on three different aspects of balancing family life that are often challenging for parents of children with autism: the siblings, the marriage, and the extended family.

When our children were first diagnosed, it was not a common occurrence for families to have more than one child with autism. We approached our subsequent pregnancies with the naïve belief that lightning would not strike twice. We recognize that our decision to have other children was not nearly as complicated as it is for parents today. We have not faced the challenges that having more than one child with autism represents.

Our worries centered on how autism would affect the lives of our typically developing children. While committed to making our family relationships work, we felt totally in the dark over how that would be accomplished. For both of us our fear overshadowed some of the joy at the births of our second children.

Maureen

Bringing Michael home from the hospital, I was paralyzed by fear and rapidly plummeting levels of postpartum hormones. All I could think was,

"What have I done?" I felt as though I had betrayed Justin by adding another child who would split our parental attentions. I felt unfair to Michael for bringing him into a family that was so unusual. I convinced myself I would be unable to provide the constant supervision that a newborn and a hyperactive five-year-old would require. I doubted my ability to cope. At a deeper level I worried I would not be able to love this new child as much as I did Justin. Even worse, I worried I might come to love Michael more. Rob caught me in my free-fall through a mixture of reassurance and humor. He reminded me of the normalcy of the postpartum blues. He reassured me that we were in this together. But he added that the men in the white jackets were on alert just in case. After a few days, the postpartum blues receded. The demanding present kept me too busy to stay paralyzed any longer.

Ann

Sarah was just over six weeks old when Eric was diagnosed. Sarah had been delivered by an emergency C-section after ten hours of labor. There was a knot in her umbilical cord that resulted in a drop in her heart rate. The doctors made a quick decision to put me to sleep and miraculously got her out in a record three-minute time. My recovery was slow and more difficult than the recovery from my C-section with Eric. Once I got home it was much harder to rest with a two-year-old and take care of a new baby. By the time of Eric's diagnosis I was finally able to walk standing upright after several weeks of walking stooped over. The doctor had just given me the go-ahead to be able to pick up Eric again when needed (which was often!).

The depression I experienced following the diagnosis was debilitating. Thankfully, I was able to continue attending to Sarah's constant newborn needs. I remember the times when I would breastfeed her in the rocking chair in her nursery. These times I would spend with her, just the two of us physically linked and alone in her darkened room, were like an escape for me. It felt like I was separated from "real life." It was a time of not having to see Eric and be reminded of all the fears I was feeling for him. I didn't have to talk to anyone about how I was doing or what the doctor had said or what we were going to do next.

Sometimes during these times of escape I would just cry and hold her and rock. Sometimes I would worry: worry about Eric and the future of my family, and worry about whether I could even do this. But I didn't worry about Sarah. I knew even at her young age that she was fine. She was different from Eric in ways I felt but couldn't name. She connected with me constantly, with her eyes, her touch, and the fleeting smiles she would give me when we were bonded together in the quiet of her nursery. She helped me feel less like a failure as a mother. Comforting her, feeding her, giving her what she needed, provided calmness and predictability to a world that otherwise felt totally out of control. Sarah was a life saver to me during this difficult time. She gave me a focus and strength that helped me swim above the surface instead of drowning. I will never forget how she helped me during that difficult time.

Four years later Philip joined our family and our life got a little more complicated. I found I was overly sensitive to any differences Sarah and Philip might have and was on the lookout for any signs of autism. I felt less worried about Sarah having autism because she was a girl. Knowing autism is less common in girls was part of it, but maybe I didn't worry because she seemed so different from Eric in so many ways. Philip was also very responsive as a baby like Sarah, but, because the incidence of autism is so much higher in boys than in girls, I was more worried about him. I was especially vigilant with his development and looked for any possible signs of autism. When he was in preschool, Philip's teacher suggested he might need speech therapy because he was stuttering slightly. I was immediately afraid that something more serious was going on. My husband helped to calm me, and, before we could schedule Philip for speech therapy, he lost the stutter on his own. He started speaking clearly and nonstop to anyone who would listen. I continued to keep an eye on him as if I were waiting for something to happen.

Despite our fears, we tried to provide the support and guidance our typical children needed to accommodate their unusual family dynamics. Here are the lessons we learned.

✻ Lesson 1: Siblings have a unique perspective

Siblings experience many of the same feelings about their brother or sister with autism that their parents do. Emotions like love, fear, frustration, pride, guilt, anger, and ambivalence may all be present. However, typically developing siblings will also have reactions that result from their own unique combination of nature and nurture. Their highly personal view of their brother or sister with autism is influenced by variables like personality, temperament, gender, birth order, and developmental stage. For example, a shy child may struggle with the public notice of his sibling's behaviors, while a more confident personality may not be embarrassed by the same situation. The experience of an older sibling who knew life before autism may be quite different from that of a younger sibling who has always known family life with autism.

Maureen

Patrick and Michael participated on a sibling panel at an Autism Society of North Carolina conference when they were teenagers. They responded to most of the questions with honesty and insight. The only questions they struggled to answer were variations on the same theme: What would life be like if Justin were a typical brother? It was a reality they had never really considered. Their responses to these questions created a light-bulb moment for me. I had grieved the loss of a "typical" family for them because I knew what it was like to grow up without a sibling with autism. Their perspective as younger siblings was different from mine. They did not grieve the loss of a typical family because our type of family was the only one they knew.

Siblings are often concerned about the causes of autism and what it means for their future and for the future of their sibling with autism. They sometimes worry about whether their own health will be affected if they "catch" the disorder.

Maureen

One day after dropping Justin off at school, Michael sat in his car seat and said, "Justin doesn't talk and is mentally retarded and is older than me, so will I be mentally retarded and not talk when I am older?" And I thought, "Here it is, THE TALK." I proceeded to earnestly explain Justin's disabilities and anticipate every possible question Michael would ever have. Then I said, "Is there anything else you want to ask me?" He took a long minute to seriously ponder the question. Then he said, "Yes. If everyone died, would there still be television?"

　　This situation reminded me how our children can keep us from taking ourselves too seriously. I was so worried about how and when to tell Michael about Justin's autism that I forgot to consider his developmental readiness to understand. It reminded me of the joke in which a father responds to his son's question of "Where did I come from?" with an elaborate sex education lecture. Puzzled, his son replied, "I thought I came from California." After my exchange with Michael, I tried to forgo the long elaborate explanations and give brief, age-appropriate information. More important, I learned to respond to the emotion-filled question behind the question. Our conversations started to include more honest answers like "I don't know," and "I know that it's hard," and "Yes, it's not fair." I stressed that as a family we would stick together and work things out the best we could.

Since parents have the most intimate knowledge of their children's unique natures, we are in the best position to help each child as an individual learn to cope in a family with autism. We can still help them experience the best that families have to offer – the knowledge that they are loved and the reassurance that their parents, despite their flaws, are always there for them.

✴ Lesson 2: Siblings may need permission to discuss their feelings

Siblings experience a wide range of emotions about living with a brother or sister on the autism spectrum. They may feel angry and resent the amount of attention the sibling requires or the disruption they may cause to family life. Siblings may be embarrassed by their brother's or sister's behaviors. They may also feel protective of their sibling and defensive toward people who don't understand autism. These conflicting emotions can be difficult for a sibling to understand and handle.

Parents can help by being sensitive to the feelings of the sibling and by giving them the opportunity to complain, ask questions, or share their concerns. We often have opportunities to discuss our own conflicting feelings about our children with other parents or professionals. Siblings usually do not have the same support system available. Siblings need to voice their feelings, both good and bad, about their brother or sister with autism. They may be reluctant to complain for fear they will anger or disappoint their parents. Siblings may be disappointed in themselves for having negative feelings about their brother or sister, making expressing these feelings out loud very difficult.

Maureen

I gave Michael and Patrick encouragement to honestly express their feelings, so long as they were positive. I wasn't so good with the negatives. I am sure throughout much of their childhood they sensed my ambivalence about hearing those negatives and modified their responses to my questions accordingly. It was not that I failed to recognize it was both normal and healthy to complain about Justin's behavior. How can you not get frustrated when Justin's reversal of days and nights kept you from getting a full night's sleep? Or angry when your bedroom gets trashed because you forgot to latch your door? Or deeply sad when you sit down for dinner each night and Justin gets up and leaves the room? Yet it was hard to hear about the difficulty of living with Justin because I was afraid their emotions were the tip of the iceberg and the negative feelings were much deeper than the positive. I was afraid it meant they did not love him.

Siblings vary in their ability and willingness to discuss their feelings about their brother or sister with autism. We can encourage the sibling to open up about their feelings by voicing our own. As parents we can set the example by admitting that we also get frustrated at times and then share how we cope with these feelings. Parents sometimes choose to speak about living with autism only as a positive experience. We may want to hide our true frustrations or sadness from our other children so as not to upset them. However, siblings need us to acknowledge at times that this life is hard and not what we had planned. Our acceptance that life with an individual with autism is challenging is an important part of adapting to the stresses of our lives and learning from them. Siblings need to acknowledge this as well so that they, too, can recognize the difficulties and then appreciate the aspects of their lives with their autistic sibling that are positive and rewarding.

Maureen

With Justin's deficits so obvious and strengths so hidden, I stressed to Michael and Patrick what Justin could do and minimized what he could not. I think it helped them appreciate his hard-fought victories in learning. In introducing Justin to a friend one day Patrick said, "Justin doesn't talk. But he is the best skater in our family" – an imitation of my habit of stressing Justin's strengths. However, my exclusive focus on Justin's strengths prevented his siblings from discussing the negatives. These subtle restrictions mirrored the restrictions I placed on myself. I rarely admitted to myself or to anyone else just how difficult our lives really were. To do so felt like a deep betrayal of Justin. I have always had difficulty reconciling negative feelings in loving relationships, as if they were mutually exclusive and not a normal part of every relationship we have. Over the years I grew more comfortable with the idea that admitting that Justin made our family life a struggle did not diminish the fact that we loved him deeply. The more honest I became with myself, the better able I was to allow Michael and Patrick to truly claim their sibling experience with Justin as their own. I knew I had made some progress when they pointed out to me that I yelled at them when I was frustrated with Justin. While I momentarily asked myself if all this honest expression of feeling was such a good thing after all, I knew their observation was correct. Voicing their complaint gave me the chance to affirm that living with Justin can be frustrating. We went on to discuss better ways to deal with my frustration than I had been using.

Sometimes initiating the discussion about the siblings' feelings is the hardest part. Creating teachable moments may be helped by using some of the various books available about having a sibling with special needs. Sometimes discussing a book about the topic or watching a movie pertaining to autism is a good way to open communication with siblings.

❋ Lesson 3: Outside support for the siblings may be helpful

Parents know that living with an individual with autism has its challenges. We know this because we are living it daily but also because of what we learn from our contacts with other families. The siblings may not have the same opportunities to learn about the experiences of other families living with autism and may not know anyone else with a sibling like theirs. Children can benefit from meeting other siblings of children with special needs.

> Sibling groups can give children an opportunity to talk about feelings such as their anger at peers for rejecting a brother or sister with autism; fear of "inheriting" autism; jealousy; and resentment of the need to compete for parental attention. Sometimes it is easier to voice these feelings outside of the family, and other children can help to affirm the acceptable nature of uncomfortable emotions. (Harris and Glasberg 2003, p.20)

Sibling support groups are now available in many communities. Parents can also help siblings by enlarging the network of adults who care about them. We found family friends, extended family members, teachers, and coaches who were all a potential source of support. Sometimes support from a counselor can also help.

Maureen

When Michael and Patrick were small, I wanted to give them the opportunity to discuss their feelings about Justin with another adult. Rob was often kept from home by the insane time demands of medical training. I knew I was giving mixed messages in the "be honest about Justin" department. I could see that as they tuned into my stress and sadness, they did not allow themselves to show much of their own. It sounds a bit crazy, but I was worried they were too good in their accommodations to our family life. In my tendency to catastrophize, I was worried about the potential for psychological problems. So I took them to a psychologist who had special expertise in the world of disabilities from both a parental and professional perspective. After several sessions, the psychologist told me they did have some issues – not with Justin but with each other! Michael thought Patrick got away with murder as the baby of the family, while Patrick resented Michael bossing him around. Those sessions with the psychologist provided some relief from my worry.

❋ **Lesson 4: Siblings need special times for themselves**

The needs of our children with autism consume much of our time. Siblings can understandably resent the amount of attention we have to give their brother or sister. One way to help siblings feel more important is to arrange time with them without the child with autism. That time can be their opportunity to get 100 percent attention from Mom or Dad. They don't have to worry about their brother or sister disrupting an outing or preventing them from doing the things they enjoy. It is also important for the parents to have this time alone with the siblings without some of the stress or anxiety that can accompany supervising the child with autism. It gives us the chance to catch up with what is going on in the siblings' lives.

Ann

When our children were younger, my husband and I made sure that there was something that Sarah and Philip had that was all their own. For Sarah it was dance. We took her to dance classes for years and enjoyed her many dance performances and recitals. Here she was the star, at least in our eyes, and we could show her how very proud we were of her. For Philip it was Boy Scouts when he was young. His father went with him on camping trips and to scout meetings and they enjoyed doing these activities together. It also filled a void for Bobby, as he could have some father/son experiences that he wasn't able to have with Eric. Later, Philip became interested in karate and we continue to support him as he works toward a black belt. These have been great opportunities for us to support their interests and to give them individual attention.

Maureen

Rob and I wanted Michael and Patrick to find after-school activities that would be all their own. We also knew that out of the world of possibilities like music lessons, scouts, art classes, or sports and clubs, our family schedule would accommodate choosing just one.

Capitalizing on their interest, we guided them to choose sports. Rob's strategy for raising boys was to "keep them tired and sweaty and in the gym." As a runner, he knew the benefits of releasing those exercise endorphins to improve both physical and mental health. We believed sports could channel their energies as young boys. We hoped sports would also be a good antidote for the raging hormones of adolescence.

My support for their participation in sports was far more selfish. I quickly discovered I now had a place where I was not in charge. Except for the occasional words of encouragement to players and words of criticism for referees, nothing beyond sitting and watching was required. Now I understood why my mom made all five of her children take swimming lessons together, well beyond the time we could swim. I became fanatical about finding respite care so I could attend Michael's and Patrick's games.

In our young family, I was worried that Justin was causing his brothers to miss out on additional after-school opportunities. Now I believe Justin did them a favor. By absorbing so much of my attention he prevented my soccer mom tendencies from over-scheduling Michael's and Patrick's time. While they enjoyed all their sports, they also enjoyed their down time. They had time to do what they wanted without having their lives overly orchestrated by an adult.

❋ Lesson 5: Every activity does not have to involve all family members

Hidden among the tasks of parenting a child with autism and making it through the ordinary activities of daily life is the challenge to find time to do things as a family. We found that picking activities that everyone could enjoy was easier when our children were little. For Maureen's family, it was outdoor activities such as swimming, skating, or hiking where Justin was physically occupied and the problem of meltdowns in public were less likely to have an impact. For Ann's family, activities such as movies, museums, and zoos provided visual enjoyment for Eric and interested the other children as well.

In most typical families as children get older and develop their individual interests, finding activities that everyone can do together is more difficult. The difference with families with autism is that as siblings go off in different directions, someone needs to stay behind with the child with autism.

Maureen

There was some regret when we decided to forgo the togetherness on every activity. As they got older, the boys reached a point where they had definite opinions about what they wanted to do. Their activities often did not interest Justin, which his behavior could make abundantly clear. We developed a "divide and conquer" parenting style that worked for us. I'd usually take Justin in one direction and Rob would take the other boys in another.

Ann

I also felt bad when we began not including Eric in some of our family activities. When he was old enough to stay at home alone, I started giving him more choice about going with us. There were times that we wanted to go to a particular movie that Eric didn't want to see, or we wanted to go to a restaurant where Eric would not eat the food they served. I would always tell Eric where we wanted to go and ask him to go with us. He usually would say "No, thank you" and was much happier staying at home. I realized that I shouldn't try to force him to participate if he didn't like what we were going to do.

As a compromise, occasionally Eric will now go with us somewhere but will do a different activity nearby that he enjoys. For example, he might go to a different movie from the one the rest of us attend. Or he might go to the mall with us but go off by himself to other stores, then we'll all meet at a certain time at the food court. Or we might pick up food he likes and take it with us to the restaurant we are going to.

Of course, there are still some activities that I don't give him a choice about participating in. One day I told Eric about a family reunion that we were hosting at our clubhouse in the neighborhood. His response was,

"Well, you know that I have autism and don't like being around large groups of people. Do I have to go?" I was impressed with his discovering how to use his autism to try to get out of something. I informed him that yes, he had to attend, but he could bring a book to entertain himself.

❋ Lesson 6: It's difficult to decide how much responsibility to place on the siblings

It can be hard to determine the amount of responsibility we should place on siblings for their brother or sister with autism. For some families there is no choice when economics and family issues require the siblings' help to make it through the day. Even when family resources are not strained, it is easy for parents to ask for too much from the siblings in helping with the child with autism. We remember growing up in more typical families where siblings are asked to "pitch in" with the responsibilities of taking care of the other children in the family who need more. With a sibling with autism, this responsibility can take on a whole new meaning. We may find ourselves asking siblings to watch over the child with autism or to help with some of the daily self-help issues. It is okay to expect all members of a family to pull their own weight, but we need to make sure that what we are asking of the siblings is appropriate for their ages and not too difficult or demanding.

Sometimes the siblings put responsibilities on themselves because of a need or desire to take care of the brother or sister with autism. They may feel a sense of protectiveness towards their sibling or a need to make life easier for their parents. While this can seem very helpful and generous of the siblings, we need to make sure the siblings aren't doing too much or feeling too much responsibility for their brother or sister. We don't want the siblings to take on adult-like responsibilities that may interfere with their enjoyment of their own childhoods. Striking the right balance can result in real benefits for both the children with autism and their siblings.

Maureen

I have never been confident about how to involve Michael and Patrick in Justin's care. Justin tended to ignore other children, including his siblings. He preferred to relate to adults, finding them not only quieter, but more accommodating and predictable as well. Finding the right balance for

Michael's and Patrick's involvement with Justin was difficult. Too much responsibility could lead to resentment (along with the potential for being pinched or scratched!). Too little involvement could lead to missed opportunities for some level of relationship.

Ultimately, I opted for Michael and Patrick to have little to no responsibility for Justin's care. I could not figure out how to involve them without significant potential for problems. Even when they were teenagers, I did not ask them to watch Justin beyond a quick errand while Justin was sleeping. I wanted to keep their involvement with Justin as positive as possible, which usually required my supervision.

I sometimes wonder if, in my attempt to not burden the siblings with Justin's care, I went too far in giving them so little responsibility. In many ways, Michael's and Patrick's childhoods ran *parallel* to Justin's, rather than *intersecting* with his. I ask myself if I worked hard enough to build areas where their relationship with Justin could be enhanced. But the advantage of hindsight is that I understand I did the best I could at the time. When my children were young, I defined a good day as one where everyone was sort of fed, sort of washed, sort of dressed, and sort of happy. I had neither the time nor the energy to manage relationships much differently. I now accept that contemplating all the roads not taken with our children is an intrinsic part of being a mother.

Fortunately, as family members age, new roads for relationships can open up. As I look at my two six-foot plus "typical" sons, I realize they are no longer children. Their futures are inextricably linked as brothers with each other, a connection that will last longer than their connection with us, their parents. As adults, Justin, Michael, and Patrick now have an opportunity to develop a relationship all their own, without the need for my orchestration.

Ann

As Sarah approached adulthood, she made the decision to attend the same university as her brother. Eric was in his third year at the university and Sarah was a freshman. When Sarah had to choose a dormitory, she and her roommate chose the same dormitory where Eric lived. There were many choices of dormitories around campus that were comparable, but Sarah wanted to live there. At first I was concerned that she had made that choice because she felt the need to be close to Eric to keep an eye on him or help him. I later realized that wasn't the case at all. I believe Sarah chose that particular place to live because she was a little nervous about leaving home, knew she might be homesick, and was comforted by having her brother near her. It was nice to witness the switch of seeing Eric as a support for her. Later, after she had lived in the same dorm with Eric for a while, I asked Sarah whether she minded Eric being in the same dorm. She answered, "No, it's Eric. He's less annoying than typical brothers."

❊ Lesson 7: Parents are powerful role models

Parents often lack confidence that they are helping their typically developing children cope with the realities that autism presents. How our typical children adjust to their lives with a sibling with autism is often beyond our parental control. We are powerless to change personality, developmental readiness, age, birth order, or gender, to make their lives less difficult. But we can take comfort in the fact that the way we relate to our child with autism can powerfully influence how the siblings cope. Parents need to recognize that what we do may be more important than what we say to our kids. Providing the siblings a role model for building a life that includes the challenges and accommodations of autism gives them an example to draw upon.

Parents often overlook all the ways we informally model and teach coping skills to our typically developing children. We respond to the autism diagnosis by pursuing information and resources. We become involved in the autism community. We reach out to others for support and contribute to supporting others. We set an example by being honest with our feelings: the good, the bad, and the ugly. We use humor to restore some perspective. We model self-care by taking time away once in a while from stressful situations. We balance responsibilities by setting expectations for everyone to contribute in some way to family life. We are also modeling to our children when we recognize the value, accomplishments, and special attributes of each family member.

At the deepest level, our daily commitment to hang in there with our difficult child may be the most important model of all – even when we feel like we are doing it badly. As Stephen Covey points out:

> In fact, the key to your family culture is how you treat the child that tests you the most. When you can show unconditional love to your most difficult child, others know that your love for them is also unconditional. (Covey 1997, p.261)

That knowledge can counterbalance a multitude of real or perceived parental failures.

✳ Lesson 8: Siblings can be a strong influence on their friends

Parents want to give their children the opportunities for all the normal experiences of childhood, especially for developing friendships. Yet remembering the cruelties shown toward children who were different in our own childhoods, we worry that the siblings may be teased or rejected by their peers.

Maureen

Over the years, I have frequently asked Michael and Patrick if other children make fun of them because of Justin. I am both curious and amazed that they deny it has ever occurred. I hope this is a sign of the times. School and community-based services for people with disabilities have increased our society's understanding and sensitivity towards disabilities from what we believed in the past. Perhaps children who now grow up in communities and schools alongside children with autism are less likely to be as fearful or negative as we were in childhood. But I think it is also Michael's and Patrick's worldview that influences their answer. I imagine that over the years people have teased or made negative comments. But by personality and perhaps by gender they tend not to notice, or care, what other people may think. If someone made an unkind or stupid remark, they would tend to consider the source and move on. They also have the good fortune to be close in age and good friends; they can shrug off other people's remarks because, at a deeper level, they know they have each other.

Not all children share this Teflon personality in which other people's opinions seem to slide off their backs. Some children have Velcro personalities, wherein remarks may initially stick, but, with some time and perspective, become easy to separate and remove. The most challenging siblings are the children with Superglue personalities where every real or perceived unkindness feels like a permanent bond. Adding in our own parental Teflon, Velcro, or Superglue personalities influences how we help our children cope.

One way we can help our children is to anticipate and avoid the potential problems whenever possible. If your child with autism falls apart at every birthday party he or she attends, maybe it's time to have a sibling birthday party without him or her. If a new friend is invited to your house for the first time, it may be helpful to have another adult or sitter available to occupy the child with autism if he or she gets upset or intrusive.

Ann

When Eric was 17 and his sister Sarah was 15, they began attending the same school for the first time in many years. Sarah was entering her first year of high school and Eric was a junior. They would be riding the bus together to and from school each day. As frequently happens, the first couple of weeks of school the bus schedule was very unpredictable. The bus was almost always late to pick up the kids at school in the afternoon to take them home. The students had to wait at the high school each afternoon, sometimes for close to an hour. When I realized this was happening, I thought about what that might be like for Eric and Sarah to wait.

I could imagine what Eric would be doing while he was waiting for the bus. He would be pacing back and forth, maybe talking to himself or flipping his fingers near his face. Then I thought about Sarah in her first year of high school trying to adjust to the transition, trying to make friends, and watching her brother pace in front of her new friends. I knew there would be questions and possible comments about Eric and that Sarah would be in an uncomfortable position. Rather than make her deal with this situation at a time when she probably felt especially vulnerable, I arranged to pick up both kids at school each afternoon. It was complicated to arrange due to my job, but I felt it was worth it to avoid a potentially difficult situation. Sometimes we need to be proactive to prevent uncomfortable situations for siblings.

We can also help siblings by welcoming their friends into our family life. While this is almost never a stress-free proposition for a parent, it is a step away from isolation and a movement toward normal childhood experiences.

Maureen

I always wanted my house to be a center of activity so the kids would not feel isolated. As my children rarely prepared new friends for the "experience" of meeting Justin for the first time, I did try to give a one- or two-sentence explanation that usually included "because of Justin's autism and mental retardation he does not talk and he makes unusual noises while he plays with his toys. He is shy around strangers and will probably keep to himself, but he is friendlier once he gets to know people better." Their friends usually looked unimpressed, shrugged off the explanation, and went back to playing.

I think in my worries about friendships for Michael and Patrick, I failed to recognize the ability of their friends to adapt to Justin's presence. Perhaps it was because they were fortunate to have friends they had grown up with or because they chose friends whose personalities were similar to their own. But the only person who seemed to be stressed about Justin's behavior in a house full of children was me.

One afternoon Patrick and a group of his friends sat around our kitchen table eating bowls of ice cream. Justin came downstairs and loudly bounded into the kitchen, ready to grab whatever food was nearest and most appealing. Without missing a beat, six kids immediately huddled over their ice cream and quickly gobbled it down. I laughed at the ability of children to adapt without parental intrusion.

I learned it did not take elaborate preparations to make our house a place where kids wanted to visit. It didn't need to be perfectly clean or to have all the latest gizmos and gadgets to occupy their time. However, I did happen upon a "friend magnet" – chocolate chip cookie mix. Purchased from our local warehouse grocery, I kept a bucket of spoon-and-bake chocolate chip cookie mix in the freezer. Serving the cookies hot, I won the hearts of my kids' friends while indulging my June Cleaver fantasy of the perfect 1950s mom. Now these friends are college students who still drop by for cookies and milk. I wish addressing other issues of family life were always this simple.

✳ Lesson 9: Parents should appreciate normal sibling behavior

It is sometimes a challenge for parents to determine which sibling behaviors are a reaction to the stress of living with a child with autism and which constitute plain old healthy, normal sibling behavior. Fighting, complaining, and angry exchanges are not always the evidence of deep-seated emotional damage or lack of a loving relationship with their autistic sibling that we worry they may be. More often it is evidence that we have allowed our children to develop lives in which they are neither miniature adults nor saints. While difficult to observe, we should feel glad about allowing them lives in which they do not always have to be paragons of patience and understanding.

Maureen

The Waltons was a popular TV show depicting the struggles and joys of a large supportive family in which all of life's challenges were usually solved by the end of the show. Each night at bedtime when the lights went out, the eldest son, John Boy, would start a chain reaction by calling out a warm good night to one of his siblings, who in turn called to another, and then to another, and down the line until Mary Ellen, Jim Bob, Ben, Jason, Elizabeth, and Erin had all been offered a sweet good night. When nighttime came to the Morrell house, we became the anti-Waltons. Justin would go to bed enamored of a toy that emitted some mind-numbingly repetitive noise. Soon after the lights in *our* house went out, voices of frustration would holler, "Justin, shut up! Mom, would you PLEASE take that toy away from him?" Or when the offending toy was the See and Say, "Justin, I don't *care* what the stupid cow says, go to sleep!" The only consolation I could give Michael and Patrick was that Justin was training them to sleep through anything, which would help them with college dormitory life.

Ann

Sometimes the behaviors of the child with autism can annoy the siblings, but other behaviors can intrigue them. When Eric was young, he would stand fairly close to the television set while watching his favorite TV shows or videos. Eric would often get excited about what he was watching and would stiffen his arms by his sides and quickly rub his fingers together. When Eric's sister Sarah was about one and a half I saw her stand next to him one afternoon while he was watching TV. She looked over at Eric while he was doing the thing he does with his hands and she watched him for a minute. She then started copying what he was doing, stiffening her arms and rubbing her fingers together. My heart sank as I had a sudden irrational thought that Sarah was looking autistic until I realized she was just trying something that she saw her brother do that he obviously enjoyed. She did it for just a minute and then stopped and sort of shrugged her shoulders as if to say "What's so great about that?" I never saw her do it again.

Other parents have shared with me similar concerns about their "typical" children imitating or picking up the behaviors of the child with autism. The other parents' stories, as in mine with Sarah, have shown that these behaviors typically don't last and the sibling eventually moves on to some other behavior that will annoy us instead of worry us.

Ann

Eric's brother and sister have been an incredible help to him over the years. They haven't spent lots of time taking care of him or working with him to teach him new skills. What has been most helpful is the time they have spent with him socially, as his siblings. Through their play (and their arguments!) they have taught him things about social rules that he could never have learned from a social skills class. Their "in your face" kind of forced social experiences helped to introduce the idea to Eric that other children can actually be fun and worth spending time with. They have taught him about what kind of clothes and music are "cool" by exposing him to their interests over the years. They have never felt like teachers, but in reality they have taught him some of the most important lessons of his life.

When Eric was first diagnosed, I thought it was crucial that he have time with his "typical" peers so that he could be exposed to their language and social behaviors. In reality, those situations were not that helpful. Eric didn't model his classmates' behaviors and he pretty much ignored them completely. The teachers were not able to set up the kind of structured learning opportunities with Eric's peers that he needed. On the other hand, his relationships with his sister and brother, because of the consistency and ongoing opportunities to connect, have been more meaningful and helpful to him than any inclusion setting in a classroom. (If there are no siblings, parents can set up play times with cousins, family friends, or older mentors that can be like sibling relationships to teach these informal lessons.)

�֍ Lesson 10: Siblings grow up

Ann

Over the years I have worried about how having a sibling with autism may have affected Eric's brother and sister. As I write this, Sarah is 20 and Philip is 15 and I am pleased by the fact that they have developed into "normal" individuals with their own unique and interesting personalities. I can now see who they have become despite, or because of, having autism in their lives. I am incredibly proud of them. They are sensitive and caring to others who are different from themselves. They respect their brother and are very proud of all he has accomplished. They do not seem resentful or maladjusted in any way, which is a great relief to me. I imagined each of them being somehow scarred for life due to the differences of growing up in a family with autism.

In some ways living with Eric has been fairly easy for Sarah and Philip, especially compared to living with a sibling with autism who has more severe behavioral issues. But having a relationship with Eric has never been easy. He does not give a lot back in terms of affection or attention. He usually prefers to be alone, and, over the years when his siblings have tried to get him to do things with them, he typically would politely say, "No, thank you." He never asks them how they are doing or what's wrong. He never wants to know what their lives are like or what they are feeling. I know he loves them but he does not show it. It makes me sad sometimes that Sarah and Philip have missed out on an emotional and reciprocal relationship with Eric, but they don't seem to mind. Like me, they have come to terms with the fact that Eric will rarely initiate a hug or sit with them just to hang out together. We all know it's not because he doesn't care about us and we have learned not to take it personally.

Sarah's choices for her future have been influenced by having Eric as a sibling. Sarah is a junior in college presently and is a double major in Spanish and psychology, planning to continue school for a Master's degree and possibly a Ph.D. She has worked with children with autism at a summer program and has provided respite for several of my friends who have children on the spectrum. She is wonderful with these children, very patient and understanding. Whatever area of psychology she decides to pursue, I know she will be especially sensitive to the clients she serves. Having a brother with autism has given her a personal perspective that will help her in her work with families and individuals with difficulties.

Both of Eric's siblings have told me that they never felt their life was especially difficult or different. In fact they are quick to remind me of their friends who grew up in families with more problems than ours. It was helpful for me to realize that indeed all families have their struggles at times and autism doesn't necessarily predetermine a sad or isolating family life.

Maureen

I shared Ann's fear that my typical children would carry deep scars from living with a brother with autism. While my worries now seem overly dramatic to me, I feared Michael and Patrick would grow up and tell me that living with Justin had ruined their childhoods. One of the difficulties in determining how well siblings manage their childhood experiences of living with a brother with autism is that you do not know much until they are older. That is when maturity gives them the words to describe and the perspective to reflect upon their experiences. So far, my children tell me their experiences did not justify my fears.

My first relief from anxiety came during a late-night conversation with Michael when he was in high school. This particular night, he was concerned about a friend who was depressed because his parents were divorcing. At the end of a long conversation, he off-handedly said, "Compared to my friends' families, our family is so normal." It was said in a tone that made normal sound synonymous with boring. Perking up at the notion that he found us normal, I asked him to explain further. He replied, "We all get along, we all like each other, and no one has any big problems." (Oh, REALLY...)

It is not that I think living with Justin did not leave some scars. Many articles about siblings indicate that siblings often have difficult feelings they do not want to share, especially with their parents. It took becoming a parent myself to face the heavy baggage of sadness and anger I carried from the difficult times in my own childhood. Just because they don't discuss their difficult feelings does not mean they do not exist. I wonder if my children will need to revisit the sadness they feel at the lack of a reciprocal relationship with their brother, or will need the chance to express the negative feelings that I tended to redirect. As I have come to understand the limits on my ability to protect my children from the hard lessons of life, I recognize that no one gets out of childhood unscarred. I would not look upon their need to revisit these issues in the future as a parenting failure. I would look upon it as a parenting success.

In the meantime, I am heartened by observing the young men of 22 and 20 that Michael and Patrick have become. They have retained maddening characteristics of normal adolescent behavior and can be lazy, forgetful, sloppy, and self-absorbed. Yet they are also kind and compassionate to the needs of others, disciplined and hard-working as students, loyal and supportive to friends and family, and "severely funny," enjoyable companions who still want to do things as a family. Despite their early baptism into learning that life can be unfair, they found the strength and spirit to survive the worst and enjoy the best. They tell me that, despite the hard times, Justin has enriched their lives and deepened their compassion. Deep down, I believe their adjustment to life results more from their nature than our nurture. But as Rob has often reminded me, the best we can ever do for our kids is provide them with limits, respect, and love. And then you just hope for the best.

Lessons for balancing family life: Siblings

1. Siblings have a unique perspective.

2. Siblings may need permission to discuss their feelings.

3. Outside support for the siblings may be helpful.

4. Siblings need special times for themselves.

5. Every activity does not have to involve all family members.

6. It's difficult to decide how much responsibility to place on the siblings.

7. Parents are powerful role models.

8. Siblings can be a strong influence on their friends.

9. Parents should appreciate normal sibling behavior.

10. Siblings grow up.

Chapter 4

Balancing Family Life
Marriage and Extended Family

Marriage

Like every other stressor that can enter a couple's life, autism tests a marriage. Any event that leads to too little sleep, too little money, too little time, too much sadness, and too much unpredictability will be a strain on a marriage.

Ann has been married for 25 years and Maureen has been married for 32 years. We have met many other parents over the years whose marriages have weathered the autism storm. We have never found one answer that explains how to keep a marriage from crumbling under the pressures of living with autism in the family. Our instincts tell us that if a marriage is strong enough before the diagnosis, chances are it will be strong enough to withstand the stresses of autism. The same would be true for marriages that can withstand job losses, a death in the family, financial difficulties, or taking care of aging parents. Parenting a child with autism, like all of these unexpected challenges, requires couples to work at keeping the marriage healthy. The following are some of the lessons we have learned.

❋ Lesson 1: Spouses may grieve differently

Mothers and fathers may have different reactions to the news that their child has autism. Some parents grieve openly and reach out for support. Some parents may hold their feelings inside and grieve privately and alone. They may refuse to believe the diagnosis or they may be driven to "fix" the problem. There is no single right way to react to this devastating news. When spouses don't react in the same way or don't agree about how to help the child, it can put a strain on the marriage.

Maureen

The differences in the way Rob and I would grieve became apparent in the delivery room when Justin was born. Because of the double-wrapped umbilical cord, Justin was sent to the nursery for observation. I immediately looked at Rob for reassurance. Instead, I felt confused and alarmed when I saw the expression of anger and pain on his face. His expression said to me, "Something is terribly wrong with this baby. I don't know if I will allow myself to get too close." I quickly assured myself that I was overreacting. I buried that observation as we buried ourselves in the relentless tasks of Justin's care, Rob's medical training, and my full-time job.

By the time we had a definitive diagnosis for Justin, we were coping with our shared sorrow in very distinct ways. Rob led with his anger. With his character defined by a strong sense of justice, he thought the magnitude of Justin's problems was supremely unfair. The irony of a special education teacher and a pediatric nurse having a child with severe disabilities felt like a cruel cosmic joke. I believe that Rob felt he had been screwed by life.

I had less inclination to expect that life would be fair. Any anger I felt was overwhelmed by a deep, pervasive sadness. Anger toward myself and other people had always made me afraid. I never really believed that relationships could be resilient enough to allow anger and love to coexist.

For years our different emotional responses created a dynamic that played out in our marriage as we tried to reach some kind of emotional balance. I read Rob's honest expressions of frustration and anger with life as a rejection of Justin. Through that emotional umbilical cord connection between mother and child, it also meant a rejection of me. As Rob over-functioned in expressing his anger, I under-functioned in recognizing and expressing my own. I felt compelled to come to Justin's defense, minimizing the difficulty of his care and putting a positive spin on our life. The more I tried to balance Rob's negativity, the more he reacted with brutal honesty. I would not understand until later the deep sadness and love for his son that his anger expressed.

Conversely, as I over-functioned in expressing my sorrow, it became harder for Rob to find room for his own. He balanced my open and frequent expressions of sadness by staying strong to take care of me. Believing that our family could not function if we both stood on our emotional last legs, he did not allow himself to fall apart. This over- and under-functioning dance became a barrier to the intimacy we had shared before Justin's arrival. As it progressed, we felt increasingly lonely.

Rob and I have rarely fought over the usual suspects in marital disputes: money, extended family, sex, or parenting styles. We fought over Justin. I was panicked that the course of our shared grief had diverged into two such separate paths. I worried that if we followed these separate paths for too long, we would not find our way back to each other. So I tried, unsuccessfully, to get Rob to feel about Justin and our family life the same way that I did. The turning point came after a long and difficult round of arguments that began over something trivial, but ended over our differences about Justin. With sadness, pain, and exhaustion in his eyes, Rob said, "Maureen, you cannot do this for me, or make me feel as you do. You need to give me some room to find my own way." Perhaps too tired to carry both his grief and mine, I finally realized he was right.

Ann

It is difficult for me to comment on the differences in grieving that my husband and I experienced following Eric's diagnosis. I don't feel confident in describing how my husband grieved because he rarely showed it. Bobby is a very sensitive, thoughtful man and feels things deeply but he rarely shows this part of himself to others. The day we first heard the word "autism," I found him crying alone in our bedroom and we held each other and cried together. After that, I never really saw him cry again about Eric. The day we found out that Eric definitely *did* have autism, Bobby was very quiet and didn't show the grief I knew he must have been feeling. Of course I was a mess and cried during the evaluation and all the way home. The physician who gave Eric the diagnosis that day later called us at home. She told me she was calling to see if Bobby was okay. I guess she was concerned because he was so quiet and didn't show any emotions. She must have read in his face what he was holding in that day. As Rob was for Maureen, so, I think, Bobby was trying to be strong for me. He knew that both of us couldn't fall apart so he let me do it. I was happy to oblige.

Perhaps more than anything else, we need to be patient with each other and communicate how each of us feels and not how our spouse should feel. We need to remember that we both are in pain and that we both love our child. We hope we can find ways to reach out to each other and be strengthened by the love and support we can give each other during a very difficult time.

❊ Lesson 2: Couples should develop realistic expectations of what they can give to one another

When you reflect on the impossible and unachievable expectations we bring to the relationship, it is no wonder that so many marriages end in divorce. When we believe that our marriage will meet *all* of our needs, we create an ideal that no marriage can possibly achieve.

To have a successful marriage, partners must exchange the unattainable fantasy marriage for the work of creating a real one. This marital task is made more complicated by the needs of our children with autism. Stress can expose all marriages' vulnerable places. As Helen Featherstone writes, "Fear threatens communication. Fatigue shortens nerves, reduces joy and tolerance, drains life of its natural color. Anger may miss its proper target and attack the relationship between husband and wife" (Featherstone 1980, p.94). In our experience, revising some of our unrealistic marital expectations helped.

Maureen

My expectations were more balanced when I was able to switch my perspective from my role as a wife to my role as a friend in my marriage. In my wife role, I carried all the "shoulds" of marriage: the "You should be able to read my mind," "We should be in agreement on Justin," or "You should want to do things my way." The wife part of me became easily resentful; it was the place where "You always..." and "You never..." resided. However, I found viewing Rob through the eyes of a friend lowered some of these unrealistic expectations. I could see things more from his perspective and find more compassion for what he was going through.

We also found that sharing every feeling and fear about our lives with autism with our spouse was not always helpful for either of us. Too close to the situation, we often felt as if we had added to each other's worries instead of relieving them. Our friends, especially other mothers, were often better sounding boards for us. It allowed us to express or vent more freely.

Ann

I think about things way too much and I want to talk about what I'm thinking, how I'm feeling, and what needs to be done. Bobby, on the other hand, is not a talker. I've always thought that I feel things strongly enough for both of us and I definitely talk enough for both of us. I am very appreciative of Bobby when I think about all the listening he has done over the years when I have needed to talk about my fears and frustrations about Eric's autism.

Bobby has been a good listener and a wonderful shoulder to cry on, but I share most of my angst about autism with my friends who are also mothers of kids with autism. They are usually more able to reciprocate with the verbal and emotional responses that I need.

Maureen

Rob and I probably personify some of the stereotypical differences in male and female responses to problems. Rob is an amazing problem solver; he is logical, analytical, and able to form his plan of action quickly. I am a processor, needing to talk all the way around an issue before I get to the bottom of what the problem is and what I need to do. We can make each other crazy when we are discussing emotional topics. I'm sure he wants to scream, "Enough already. We discussed it *ad nauseum*. Let's move on to some resolution." On the other hand, I want to know I am being heard; I am not necessarily seeking answers. Over the years, we have learned to be more direct in asking for what we need from each other.

Another unrealistic expectation is that all issues are resolvable. All couples fight. A recent *New York Times* article titled "The Key to a Lasting Marriage: Combat" states that, according to a growing body of research, there is no such thing as a compatible couple. In 69 percent of both happy and unhappy marriages, some disagreements are never resolved. Rather than trying to resolve the irresolvable, experts in marital therapy believe that "what tends to predict the future of a relationship is not what you argue about, but when you do argue, how you handle your negative emotions" (Stout 2004, p.D8).

Maureen

I would like to claim that Rob and I always employed the best communication skills when we disagreed: that we listened, without interrupting, to understand the other's point of view; that we replaced the "You always..." and "You never..." phrases with "I need..." or "I feel..."; that we avoided patronizing tones of voice and nonverbal behavior, such as looking disgusted and rolling our eyes (skills I have raised to an art form); and that we focused on the problem at hand and did not drag in every past hurt. I would like to be able to say that, but it would be a lie. We were too young, too hurt, too worried, and too different in our grief over Justin to always fight fair.

But we did stumble upon two strategies that were often successful in helping us resolve our disagreements. The first was to recognize that sometimes what we argued about was not the real problem. The real problem fueling the fight was the fact that we were exhausted and needy at the same time. It was important for us to remind each other that, at least temporarily, we had nothing left to console the other. Our tanks were empty. It helped to lower expectations about what we could give and get from each other at those low energy times.

The second strategy was so helpful that it was elevated to the level of a rule. The rule was: Never go to bed still angry with each other. From experience, I can testify that this is a hard rule to follow. Not allowing ourselves to sleep on an argument consigned us to many sleepless nights. But clearing the air between us kept disagreements to a size we could manage. It prevented silence and anger from making arguments loom larger than life.

❋ Lesson 3: Responsibilities can be divided based on strengths

Taking care of a young child with autism can be a physically and mentally exhausting task. In addition to the physical care of the child it involves being knowledgeable about the disability and being able to advocate appropriately for the child. Ideally, couples should share these responsibilities so that neither partner becomes too overwhelmed and exhausted.

Each of us has our own strengths and weaknesses. In the ideal world, if one parent tends to be more patient and has better teaching skills, that parent may need to be more involved in teaching the child self-help skills. If one parent feels more comfortable in the advocating role, that parent may need to be the one who makes the phone calls and attends meetings with the schools. Every responsibility does not have to be shared by both parents but can be designated to the parent who has more skills or interests in that particular area. In the real world, however, it is a significant challenge for any couple to figure out how to divide the responsibilities in a way that is efficient and fair. The two parents simply may not have equal amounts of time and energy to invest in caring for their child with autism.

Ann

I used to get angry sometimes that my husband was not as involved in advocating for our son as I would have liked. I was the one who was making the phone calls and making sure Eric's needs were being met at school or in therapies. I was the one who was trying to learn everything I could about autism and attending the support groups and workshops.

I realized early on that it wasn't that my husband wasn't as devoted to our son or didn't care about his services. He was just as invested in helping him as I was. I realized that attending conferences and support groups was not his "thing." I loved attending any forum where I could meet other parents and learn more about autism. I personally needed to be involved at that level and needed to reach out to other parents for support. My husband did not feel that same need. He was also working a stressful job that was not very flexible, and participating in meetings and conferences was not easy and added to his stress level. I was the appropriate person to be the main advocate for Eric at school because I was good at it and had more interest, knowledge, and time to help. It worked for our relationship for me to be the primary advocate and to share what I was learning with my husband. We made the major decisions about Eric's services together and he would attend all the important meetings with me.

When things were especially overwhelming at the beginning, I would be inspired and encouraged by anything positive I would hear about Eric. The teacher or occupational or speech therapist might tell me something new Eric had accomplished that day and I would feel so much better. I realized that my husband was not getting the same opportunity to hear those encouraging words from the professionals. I was the one who watched through the two-way mirrors as Eric made improvements or accomplished something challenging. Bobby needed to feel hopeful, too, and I made sure that I remembered all the little successes and promising comments the teachers and therapists told me so I could repeat them to Bobby. I also made a point of occasionally working with Eric one-to-one during the evenings so Bobby could see all the neat things we were doing and how much Eric was learning.

Maureen

I remember that "spouses" was always a lively topic for our mothers' support group. Our discussion would often deteriorate into a litany of our frustrations over what our spouses were not doing to help. I usually had something to contribute to this discussion. Rob's schedule at the hospital legitimately consumed long hours. In his honesty, even at his own expense, he had made matters worse by admitting that some nights he worked even longer because he could not face the chaos at home. While I was relieved to be able to be a full-time caregiver, I was resentful of doing so much by myself. I was frequently frustrated that when he did help, he did not do it correctly (a.k.a. my way). As we went around the room at the mothers' group, with each complaint an echo of the former, Ann created a teachable moment for me when she said, "I've given up being angry with Bobby. I just think I do this stuff better than he does."

She went on to explain that due to time and temperament she was the better one to take the lead in Eric's care. Her insight spoke to my situation as well. I was blaming Rob for not helping more, when the reality was he worked 15-hour days. He came home at the "arsenic hour" at night when Justin was usually in total meltdown mode. It seemed that for many years he never really got to see Justin at his best. As the primary caregiver, I got to see Justin's progress and not just his problems. I got support from the people and programs that helped Justin. Ann's story helped me realize the issue was not that Rob was not helping. He was doing all that he could to provide necessary financial and emotional support. The issue was our family needed more help than we both could provide. With both of us stretched to the max, it started me on the path of finding additional care providers to help our family.

❋ Lesson 4: It is important to make time for yourself as a couple

Living with autism can become so all-encompassing that we forget to take the time for ourselves or for our marriage. Free time is hard to find, and when we have the precious opportunity to do something for ourselves, we tend to choose the basic necessities such as sleeping, eating, or bathing. Finding the time and energy to spend an evening with your spouse without children may seem like a luxury you don't deserve. But you deserve it – and marriages need it. Husbands and wives need to have the pleasure of an occasional time together without worrying about the responsibilities that can overwhelm their daily lives.

Going out together as a couple involves finding someone you trust to take care of your child. That is usually not easy. We worry about finding anyone who can take care of our child with autism as well as we can, or who can keep our child safe. No matter how hard it may be to find appropriate respite care, it is important to do it if at all possible. If you have friends or family members who are offering to help in some way, take them up on it. Let them watch your children so you can have an evening out. Explore the respite care services that are offered in your area. It will not only be good for your marriage, but it can give your child the new experience of adjusting to a different caregiver.

Even if it is a brief dinner out or running errands together, it is important to have the break and spend time with each other as a couple. It helps to decide ahead of time what we want these "breaks" to provide. It may be a romantic time together or a time to discuss important issues without the distractions at home. Some parents may want to set a rule that the "A" word is not to be used during the time out. The time away from home may also be used for sharing a common interest such as working out together, or going to sporting events, or attending movies. Whatever the choice, we need to use this time to listen to each other and give each other the individual attention we both deserve.

Ann

During the early years, my husband and I rarely had time with each other without the kids. His work kept him very busy and my days taking care of a new baby and taking Eric to his many therapies were pretty exhausting. By the time the kids went to bed at night, we had little energy left. I missed my husband and needed time when I was not in a mother's role. We started planning a date one night a week where we would get a sitter and leave the house for a few hours. We would go out to dinner or go to a movie. It was heaven and it became something to look forward to each week. Sometimes we just went to a fast-food restaurant or walked around the mall. It wasn't what we were doing that was important, but just the fact that we were having the time to talk and be together without the children.

My husband and I recently went away on a vacation together to celebrate our twenty-fifth wedding anniversary. Throughout our marriage we have taken trips together without our children. When the children were young it was harder, but we still managed to get away, even if it was only for a weekend. These times away rejuvenated our marriage and gave us time for each other, something that was often missing during our hectic times at home. Everything felt easier and more tolerable when we returned. The children would always miss us, but it was good for them, especially Eric, to have other people taking care of them with different routines and ways of doing things.

I know this is very difficult to do for most families with children with autism. We had the advantage of having family locally who were willing to help take care of the children. Many families do not have that luxury. Finding good caregivers may be next to impossible for overnight trips, but it's worth the effort to try!

Maureen

Like Ann and Bobby, preserving time for us was both a challenge and a salvation for our relationship. Whether it was enforcing (to the degree possible) regular bedtimes for our children so that we had time alone each night, or arranging for time away from home, finding time to reconnect with each other was one of the most important things we did for our marriage. It helped me see beyond the stress and strains of our life and remember why I still both liked and loved this man.

Extended family

Family relationships are frequently complicated and everyone has a history of good and bad experiences with family members. Having a child diagnosed with autism can further complicate these relationships. If we are close to an extended family member, chances are that relationship will continue to thrive even after the autism. However, if the quality of the relationship has always been tenuous, autism can make it more so. There may be disagreements about the actual diagnosis, or disagreements about the parenting style and choices for therapies. Because of our child's behaviors, we may have to limit visits to family or the child's involvement in family functions. Extended family members who don't see our child frequently or don't understand the day-to-day difficulties of taking care of a child with autism may not understand the decisions we make.

Grandparents of a child with autism have it especially hard. Not only do they grieve for the grandchild with autism, but they also grieve for their own child who is struggling. They may desperately want to help but don't know how, or they may be restricted by distance or health issues. Parents may have difficulty asking for help, or letting their loved ones be involved in the personal struggles they may be experiencing. Here are the lessons we learned about involving our extended family.

✳ Lesson 1: You may need to adjust your expectations

"Achieving success by lowering expectations" is the company motto of Despair.com. It is also a good mantra for promoting positive family relations. Families are such a complex mixture of heredity, history, and unique personalities. There are so many things about family relationships that are beyond our control. About the only thing we can control is the level of our own expectations.

Maureen

I was fortunate in that, for the first five years of Justin's life, we lived close to my brothers and sister. I did not expect them to have any difficulty welcoming Justin to our extended family. Accepting differences in people (except perhaps political ones) is a longstanding tradition in my family. I knew without hesitation that they would close ranks around us and provide any support we requested.

I did not know what to expect from Rob's family. When Justin was born, we were living in the Midwest, while Rob's family members lived on the two coasts. I did not doubt that they loved us and would help where they could. But I worried about how they would feel about Justin.

My greatest concern was with Rob's parents as our early relationship with them had been strained. For a whole host of reasons Rob's parents were opposed to his earlier choice of a special education career. I worried about how they'd react to a "special ed" grandchild of their own. I protected myself by keeping my expectations low.

What they were able to provide exceeded my expectations. Their love and their loyalty towards family helped them move beyond their initial struggle to accept Justin as one of their own. They expressed their love and concern and kept us in their daily prayers. They offered financial assistance which eased some of the stress in our family.

But it was sad that Rob's parents never came to know Justin very well. They never really got over seeing him as "poor Justin," and never saw our life without tragic overtones. I knew that they felt we should place Justin outside our home. Luckily, they had the good manners (and good sense) not to tell us what they thought we should do.

In the end, their view of our lives did not cause me much pain. Because I did not rely on them as my main source of emotional support, I did not expect more than they were able to give.

❊ Lesson 2: Extended family members may benefit from education about the child's autism

Extended family members typically are not knowledgeable about the autism spectrum. Not only can they benefit from learning more about autism, they also need to learn more about how autism affects their family member. Every child with autism is different, and learning how autism affects their loved one can help family members better understand what parents may be going through. We can explain to family members about the child's difficulties and strengths. It is also helpful to sometimes share literature on autism with them. There are many books available as well as quick factsheets about the disorder from websites on autism. We can also share the diagnostic or therapy reports about our child with family members who may be interested. Keep in mind that the clinical descriptions in these reports can sometimes be emotionally difficult to read. Choosing what to share with the extended family members should be done carefully and with consideration of the family member's possible emotional response and their level of interest and knowledge.

One of the best ways to help a family member learn about the child's autism is by having them spend time with the child. That may not be easy if the family member lives far away. Frequently it is hard for families with a child with autism to travel to visit relatives when the child doesn't do well out of the normal routines. It may be easier for relatives to visit the child in his or her home. Many of the disagreements about the diagnosis or about treatment choices may arise because the extended family members don't completely understand the complicated nature of our children. Spending time with our children in their home environment can be very enlightening for family members. We can invite the relative to observe the child at a therapy session or see the child in a school activity. Relatives might also benefit from attending a support group for families with autism.

Ann

As I mentioned previously, we were very fortunate that Eric's grandparents lived nearby. I found that it meant a great deal to them to be included in my learning process as I was trying to understand autism and how to help Eric. I would share many of the reports and evaluations on Eric with his grandparents. I gave them articles I read about autism that I thought would be meaningful to them. I would take them with me to occasional support groups and conferences. They watched me work with him at home and were able to observe him sometimes at occupational and speech therapy sessions. I think it helped them understand Eric, and it made them more accepting and supportive of us in our parenting decisions. They also felt more involved, and more capable of helping us and Eric.

Maureen

I have always had trouble deciding how much information about Justin to share with our families. At first we had too little information to go on. The question of how his birth injuries would affect his future development was unclear. I was almost superstitious in not wanting to tell anyone, even family, about all my fears. Receiving a diagnosis did not provide all the answers. We learned that Justin's disabilities were severe, but did not know how his autism would play out. At this time I was struggling with my own learning curve about autism. I was unsure how to explain this confusing child to our family when I did not understand this mysterious disorder myself.

Probably an even greater deterrent to discussing Justin with family was how I hated being the messenger of bad news. Adding worry and sadness to their lives increased the weight of the sadness I carried in my own. When I assumed the messenger role, it drained too much emotional energy from me. I needed all of my emotional reserves to take care of the family at hand.

So, unlike Ann, I did little to educate our family about autism. I decided that to understand Justin, well…you just had to be there. For our family members who lived far away, I gave general answers to questions but rarely got into the details. They had few opportunities to know him because of his limited tolerance for travel. Family members who visited or lived nearby learned about Justin's particular brand of autism by spending time with him. By including him in their lives, they came to understand and accept the whole child. They tell me that knowing Justin has taught them a lot and that he has enriched their lives. I know that their acceptance of him has certainly enriched ours as well.

✳ Lesson 3: Parents should accept help if it helps

Accepting help from family members can be complicated. Part of the developmental stage of a young family is to establish their independence by separating from their families of origin. Just when you have started that separation, a child with autism may require you to take a step back to your family for support. How to negotiate accepting help and maintaining independence is a tricky balance.

Maureen

I did not turn to my extended family for emotional support, at least not the kind of support that involved processing the experience of having Justin as part of my life. It was not that our extended family was unable or unwilling to help. It was my own reluctance to burden anyone else. I was the eldest daughter and middle child in my family. I was used to the giving and not the receiving end of support. To do otherwise took me out of my comfort zone. Looking back I think I did a disservice to my family and myself by not being more open. But I also recognize that I probably did the best I could at the time.

Yet our siblings showed their support in many practical and generous ways. Both families financially supported the programs that help people with autism. Through her offers to babysit, my sister was my weekend salvation. My brothers and sisters-in-law always included us in their family events. When it came time for our family reunion, they insisted on a North Carolina beach so Justin would be able to attend. Since our ability to travel was limited, my brother-in-law's family came to us. Their financial generosity over the years gave us opportunities for vacations we would never have had otherwise.

✳ Lesson 4: Sometimes you have to know when to say when

We may try everything we can think of to convince a family member that the diagnosis is correct, and still find that they continue to believe there is no problem. Or we may try every strategy we can think of to help a family member accept the child for who he or she is, only to find that it's to no avail. We hear other parents talk about the family member who thinks the problem with the child is due to poor discipline strategies. Or the family member who, ten years after the diagnosis, still won't spend time with the child or treats him or her differently from other children in the family. Adversity does not necessarily strengthen connections within the family.

Sometimes we have to stop worrying about how to change a family member's viewpoint and just learn when to say when. We want our family to support us and to love our child for who he or she is. But we don't need the added stress of dealing with relatives' ignorance or stubbornness when we have tried everything we can to involve them and educate them about our child. Some family relationships are just too fragile to withstand the challenges that autism brings, and, despite our best efforts, the relationship may not survive. It's sad but it's necessary in some situations for parents to make the decision that allowing a particular family member to be involved is not healthy for the child or for the family. Our energies may be more productive when directed towards building on those family relationships that are supportive and add to our lives.

Sometimes "saying when" to our family relationships can be temporary. We forget that relationships can change over time. During the days when we are raising our children, we have our hands full of obligations of family and work. There is a limit to what we can offer to anyone outside our nuclear family. But when the child-rearing days are over there can be new opportunities to re-establish new kinds of family relationships.

Maureen

I have been surprised and delighted that as our families have grown up there are more opportunities for extended family members to be involved in Justin's life. As his cousins have become adults, they are able to come to visit. They follow the explosion of autism information in the media and frequently email me articles that provide the latest autism information. They are curious about Justin's life and ask questions about his past and his present. They donate to the causes that improve his life and the lives of other individuals with autism. As Rob and I age, I am encouraged by the chance to expand the circle of family members who care about Justin and may be able to offer him support in the future.

Lessons for balancing family life

Marriage

1. Spouses may grieve differently.

2. Couples should develop realistic expectations of what they can give to one another.

3. Responsibilities can be divided based on strengths.

4. It is important to make time for yourself as a couple.

Extended family

1. You may need to adjust your expectations.

2. Extended family members may benefit from education about the child's autism.

3. Parents should accept help if it helps.

4. Sometimes you have to know when to say when.

Chapter 5

Advocating for Our Children

The diagnosis of autism spectrum disorder catapults parents into the role of advocates. In order to find the support and services our children require we face the daunting task of navigating school, health, and human services systems. At a time when our autism learning curve is at its steepest, it becomes our job to explain, interpret, defend, and promote our children. Parents can easily feel unprepared and overwhelmed.

When obstacles loom larger than life, breaking the task down to manageable pieces can help us take action. In advocacy, the first step is to find the professionals who can help. Over the years we have worked with professionals whose skill and compassion vastly improved the quality of life for Eric and Justin and for our families. We have also met some professionals whose lack of skill and compassion made our lives miserable. As new advocates, it was sometimes hard to tell them apart.

Maureen

I tended to view all the professionals as experts. Like the good Catholic schoolgirl I once was, I respected their authority and accepted their view as the gospel truth. My relief at having someone to help sometimes obscured an objective evaluation of their expertise. Rob was more discerning and objective. I remember taking Justin to speech therapy sessions that always ended in massive meltdowns for both Justin and me. Rob knew that these sessions upset me and decided to come to observe.

After 15 minutes he said, "Why are *you* feeling terrible about these speech sessions? It isn't Justin's fault. She's a lousy therapist. She sits across the table with perfect hair, perfect nails, perfect makeup, and perfect clothes and has all the warmth of a fish. If I were Justin, I would throw a fit as well. We need to find someone who actually likes working with our child."

As we grow in the role of an advocate, we get better at judging which professionals can offer the knowledge and support that we need and who we can trust. In the following we will first examine ways to build positive relationships with professionals and then how to manage the conflicts that can arise. We will also offer some advice for what we did when our advocacy efforts failed. Finally, we will examine what qualities distinguished the best professionals who worked with our families and how these qualities served as our standard for the "best practices" professionals can use in working with parents.

I. Building positive relationships with professionals

To create positive relationships between parents and professionals takes time and effort, which may be in short supply with the constant demands at home. But the investment of time and energy to establish a good relationship is minimal compared to the time and energy that will be required to fix a failing one. Here are the lessons we learned that helped us build positive relationships with professionals.

❊ Lesson 1: Decide what you want for your child

The best professionals in the world will not be able to help if they do not know what assistance we need. So before the relationship begins, we need to preserve time for reflecting on what kind of life we want for our children. This is a challenging task because so much of the future is still unknown: what expectations are reasonable, what achievements are possible, what strengths will emerge, what preferences will develop, what advances in the autism field will make life easier to manage. Our vision for our children's lives changes and modifies as answers to these questions begin to reveal themselves. Effective advocacy requires us to stay open to the possibilities for the future, while meeting the real needs in the present.

The educational and treatment plans we develop with professionals need to reflect the whole child and not just the diagnosis. Developing a well rounded and written profile of our child can help guide both short-term and long-range planning efforts. Some questions to consider include: "What are my child's strengths? What are his challenges? What are his interests? What are his most admirable qualities? What helps him to learn? What are his hopes and his fears and vision of his future?"

Maureen

The Individualized Educational Plan (IEP) process is sometimes an example of the Law of Unintended Consequences. It started out as an important planning tool for parent–professional cooperation, based on the individual needs and abilities of the child. Yet, as more and more regulations have been added to assure its correct implementation, the IEP has become less of a planning tool and more of a compliance document. Using a student profile can help keep the IEP rules, regulations, educational jargon, and paperwork from taking the focus off our child. I used the profile to remind the entire IEP team that, red tape aside, Justin needed to be the center of our attention.

❋ Lesson 2: Children should participate in advocacy as they are able

Some children will have more ability to participate in advocacy efforts than others. Some will not be able to advocate for themselves at all. Of course parents must consider the child's level of understanding and ability to communicate, but it is possible to help many children develop the self-advocacy skills that they will need as adults. The more involved students are in the IEP process, the better prepared they will be to advocate for themselves in the future. We can begin preparing our children very early for self-advocacy by helping them understand their differences and how to ask for help. We can make sure very young children know why they may need help and who is there to help them at the school. We can help our children understand that all children learn differently and that everyone has strengths as well as challenges.

We may want to protect our children from hearing others discuss their problems. Their weaknesses and difficulties are going to be discussed during IEP meetings, but so will their strengths and interests. We have to overcome the tendency to protect them from uncomfortable discussions and instead try to anticipate their future and their need to advocate for themselves when they are older. Students with autism should be involved in their IEP meetings at the level that is appropriate. Some students may not be able to attend the meetings, but, with the help of teachers or parents, they can make choices ahead of time that can be shared at the meetings. Some students may only be able to attend the meetings for a short while, maybe just to meet the members of the team. Students can read a prewritten statement at the meeting about what they like or don't like or what is difficult for them. Whatever the level of participation, it is important that our students understand that the IEP team cares about them and will work to help them be successful in school.

Schools typically do not require the student to attend the IEP meetings. The student may not officially be invited to a meeting until the Transition Plan meeting that takes place in high school. Parents may need to suggest that the student attend IEP meetings. Students will need to be prepared beforehand about why the meeting is happening, who will be there, and what will be discussed. Involving the students in advocacy may seem like a great deal of work, but it will be worth it to help them understand their strengths and needs. They can also learn to interact with people who are important to their chances for success.

Ann

I was guilty of not getting Eric involved early enough in meetings about his school services. It always seemed easier to do it without him. I also thought it would bother him to hear people talking about his weaknesses. One of the first meetings he participated in was his Transition Plan meeting when he was in high school. All the regular players were there: his occupational therapist, one of his teachers, the assistant principal, the guidance counselor, the exceptional children's representative, and my husband and I. I had also invited several people who were not normally included: his grandmother, his supervisor at his volunteer job at a local museum, a vocational rehabilitation representative, a TEACCH therapist who had known him since he was first diagnosed, and the transition specialist for our school system. It was a large group and we were all sitting around a big table, with Eric included. The introductions began and everyone said their names and how they were connected to Eric, such as what agency they represented or what their job was. When it got to be Eric's turn he said, "My name is Eric Palmer and I have autism." I was surprised because I had never heard Eric announce that so emphatically. Later when I asked him about it he said that everyone else was introducing themselves with a title after their name and that was all he could think of.

Several years later when Eric and I had our first meeting with disabilities services at his college, I quickly learned the necessity of his knowing how to advocate for himself. The disabilities services provider was very kind and helpful but she directed all of her questions to Eric. After years of being Eric's primary advocate with the school, it was somewhat of a shock to me that she was not asking for my input. Legally, because Eric was over 18 and his own guardian, she needed the requests for services to come from him. She would ask him if he needed a certain accommodation for a class such as hard copies of notes and he would answer, "I don't know. Mom, what do you think?" I realized then that I should have started earlier involving him more in the planning of his services and supports in school. He was not prepared for the level of self-advocacy that college requires.

✳ Lesson 3: Parents need to develop advocacy skills

Collaborative parent–professional relationships create the best environment for helping our children with autism to succeed. Parents claim their role as equal partners in the support process when they act in ways that advance a collaborative approach. We can increase the likelihood of achieving successful relationships with professionals by using many of the same techniques that help us succeed in our relationships at work and at home: by bringing honesty, integrity, openness, and respect to the process. What follows are some practical strategies to incorporate these principles into positive interactions with professionals.

(a) Meet the teacher and other professionals before the program begins

Ann

Much of the advocating I had to do over the years for Eric was done before each school year started. Eric didn't have behavior issues and didn't require special supports in the classroom that would require my advocacy efforts during the school year. It was the advocating I did at the first meeting with his new teachers that usually was crucial and, if successful, could keep me from needing to advocate as much during the year. At the first meeting I had to sell my son; convince them that he could do the work with minimal effort on their part and convince them that he was not going to suddenly change into a student who was impossible to handle. Sometimes I had to convince them that he did indeed have autism and did need the supports that were available.

I also had to sell myself. In order for them to feel comfortable communicating with me about how Eric was doing during the school year, they needed to see me as a non-threatening parent who was not too pushy or expecting too much. I let them know how much I supported them and that I was willing to help in the classroom in any way they needed me. I stated clearly that they could contact me at any time with questions about Eric or his autism. I mainly wanted them to see me as a partner, not a threat.

Maureen

Rob and I always visited the principal of a new school before the school year started. It was one of the few times that I made an appointment for "Dr. and Mrs. Morrell" and we dressed the part. It was my attempt to establish us as reasonable, thoughtful, and desirable parents to have at the school. I hoped to fix that image in the principal's mind when the inevitable meeting about Justin's behavior was requested.

(b) Share information about your child

Review your child's student profile with the professional and discuss your child's strengths, needs, interests, and learning style. Be open and honest, but also make sure you express any questions or concerns you may have about confidentiality issues.

(c) Be an ambassador for your child

In addition to needs and concerns, be sure to add some of the unique and endearing qualities you find in your child. Share some of your hopes and your dreams for your child.

(d) Provide the "Autism 101" on your child

Your special education teacher may know about autism, but you know your child. If your child is in the regular classroom you may need to educate the teacher about both autism and your child. Share practical advice and tips for preventing problems. Help anticipate some of the problems that may arise and offer practical suggestions for managing them. This information is especially helpful for new professionals who are in that period of culture shock between the theoretical knowledge they learned in school and the practical realities of working with children in the field.

Maureen

I was conscientious about trying to prepare the professionals for problems that might arise. Being an experienced catastrophizer, the challenge was to give the most pertinent information and not overwhelm them with every possible scenario ("Now, in the event of a nuclear war, Justin may need to..."). So, knowing that Justin's behavior was the most limiting variable in his life, I spent most of my time sharing the practical ways of preventing problems and managing his behavior. For example, "Justin is more likely to do what you say when you use a humorous tone of voice. He tends to hit people who give him instructions with an authoritative tone of voice." "Justin's a sucker for smiles, back rubs, and silly songs." "If you seat Justin at the end of the cafeteria table, he is less likely to grab food from someone else's plate." "I find that when giving him extra time to process what I say, it makes it easier for him to respond." "When Justin starts to get upset, finishing the task quickly and taking a power walk can calm him down."

With so many suggestions to convey to the professional, it can be difficult to decide how to provide the information in a usable form. Written suggestions are helpful. But I found a picture really is worth a thousand words. Using a video was one of the best vehicles for sharing ways to work with Justin. We discovered the idea when we moved to three different school districts while Justin was in elementary school. One of his creative teachers did a video to take to his new school that included interviews with all the professionals who worked with him. The video incorporated footage from both the good and the not-so-good in his typical day in the classroom. The teacher narrated a running commentary over the footage to explain what and how they were teaching in that particular scene. She peppered the screen with lots of suggestions that she found invaluable. The video not only conveyed important strategies for working with Justin, it also had the added benefit of showing that, despite all his challenging ways, he won the hearts of the professionals who worked with him.

Ann

Sometimes parents' advocacy efforts need to be directed towards helping the teacher know how to prevent possible behaviors and how best to respond to the behaviors when they happen. My advocacy had more to do with keeping Eric from being ignored. For most of his school years, Eric had no disruptive behaviors in the classroom. On the contrary, he would never break any rules. My concerns for Eric in the classroom were that he would "get lost in the shuffle" or not know what to do. He had difficulty focusing sometimes and would need to be redirected to pay attention. He would sometimes miss the teacher's instructions and then not ask for help. Over the years it always helped Eric if teachers would check now and then to see if he understood or would repeat instructions for him.

I was also concerned that other students would be mean to him or take advantage of him. He was always alone because he didn't have friends and he had self-stimulatory behaviors that drew attention to his differences. I knew bullies would see him as a perfect target. Each year before school started I would try to emphasize to the teachers my concerns and ask that they keep an eye on Eric, especially during unstructured time in the classroom and on the playground. I would also ask them to try to find another student in the class who seemed willing to help Eric as a "peer helper." In a busy classroom with numerous students requiring attention from the teacher, it was necessary for me to emphasize Eric's special need for extra attention.

Ann

When I wanted to educate new teachers about my son, I used a "Student Information Sheet" (see Appendix A), available from the Exceptional Children's Assistance Center (ECAC). It is a one-page questionnaire that can be completed by a student's previous teacher or someone who has worked with the student and knows him or her well. The questions are very positive and include what was rewarding about working with the child and what the child's strengths and interests are. However, it also covers the child's difficult behaviors and strategies that might be needed to deal with them.

I found that teachers appreciated this short, easy-to-read information sheet. It helped prepare them for what it would be like working with the student and what their responsibilities might include. They also appreciated getting this information from other teachers with direct experience working with the student (as opposed to information from a parent). It is especially useful when a student is transitioning to a new school. I had teachers and therapists from Eric's elementary school complete the form and I made sure each of his new teachers at the middle school got it.

(e) Get to know the professional

Take time to find out about the professional's background and experience. Learn about the good and bad relationships he or she has had with parents and what made the difference. Share your expectations of the parent–professional relationship and ask them to share theirs. Decide the best time and method for communications.

(f) Pick your battles

Sometimes parents have to choose what is worth fighting for. It is important to prioritize the resources and supports that would benefit your child, and to concentrate your advocacy on obtaining the items that seem to offer the greatest benefits. When pursuing a particular resource or support, parents have to view realistically the chances of getting what they are asking for. They should take into consideration the time, effort, and possible strain on the parent–professional relationship that fighting that particular battle can require. They then have to decide if the goal is worth the effort and time it will require to pursue it. If a parent is unclear, asking advice from his or her trusted advisors may help.

Ann

In high school Eric was scheduled to take a required physical science course. At the beginning of the school year we arranged a meeting with Eric's teachers to discuss autism and what his needs might be for that year. The physical science teacher did not attend nor did she respond in any way to the invitation or explain why she couldn't attend. Soon after the start of the class Eric started bringing home low test scores and homework grades and I tried to contact this teacher to discuss it. I emailed her and called her and she never responded to the messages I left. When I mentioned to another school staff member that I wasn't getting responses from my messages, she was not surprised. She told me that this particular teacher had previously been involved with some other teachers in a lawsuit brought against the school by a group of parents of students with learning disabilities.

From this information and the teacher's unwillingness to respond to my attempts to contact her, I concluded that she was not willing to be involved in any way with students with special needs. In my opinion she was not going to be convinced that working with Eric would be easy and rewarding. She obviously had had enough. I could have followed legal procedures to try to force her cooperation, and maybe I should have. But I decided that this was not a battle I wanted to fight. I didn't feel it would make a big difference in Eric's success in school. Instead we removed Eric from this teacher's class and placed him in another class.

(g) Share information about issues that may be affecting your child

Any stresses at home such as divorce, illness, births, or deaths as well as stresses at school may require the professionals to provide additional support for your child.

(h) Offer to help

Give whatever time, talent, and financial resources you are able to give.

(i) Offer moral support

Acknowledge when you think the professionals are doing a good job with your child. Their job satisfaction certainly does not come primarily from their salary or their working conditions. Giving genuine praise for the positive things the professionals do for your child can boost their morale. Professionals who feel good about themselves and their job will work better with our children.

Ann

As a sign of my support for the teachers and school personnel who would be helping my child, I always brought something yummy to the meetings. Typically I would bring brownies. I found it helped break the ice to start the meeting and it was a gesture of my support and appreciation for what they were doing or would be doing for my child. It was a small gesture but I think it was a good start to building trust between us.

❈ Lesson 4: It helps to get organized

The advocate role carries with it an incredible paper trail. In order to keep track of all the numerous meetings, people, and information that cross our paths, parents should develop a record-keeping process that is functional and makes life easier. Keeping good records can be especially important if more complicated advocacy efforts must be used.

Everything should be in writing. All communications in person and by telephone should be documented and include information about who you communicated with, when, and what was discussed. Parents should also send a follow-up letter after a conversation or meeting that summarizes what was decided, who will do what, and by when.

All reports and correspondence need to be dated and organized so that they can be easily referenced. Any requests for services should also be in writing with copies for the parents and professionals. When preparing for upcoming meetings, collect all the information that is necessary to bring to the meeting and develop a list of questions or topics you may want to cover.

Meetings are an inescapable and often maddening fact of life in advocating for our children. When they are poorly planned, overly long, and unfocused, everyone involved can get testy. Without adequate preparation, meetings create more disagreements than they resolve. Be sure the purpose of the meeting is clear to all parties and that sufficient time has been allotted to accomplish its purpose. A good question to ask at the onset is, "What do we hope to accomplish by the time this meeting is over?" Define the purpose of the meeting. Is it to share information, develop a plan, solve a specific problem, or evaluate the plan thus far? In our experience, parents and professionals try to cover way too much ground in a single meeting. Each team member doing assigned preparation before, and homework after, may help meetings serve their purpose without generating conflict.

Ann

When it would get close to the time for Eric's yearly IEP meeting, I found myself getting "revved up" and overly organized. I became obsessed with preparing for the meeting: gathering all the necessary paperwork, making lists of issues to discuss, and gathering examples of Eric's work. I would be energized much like a soldier preparing for battle. I was in my "Super Advocate" role and I prided myself on being as prepared as possible. As I look back at those times and try to analyze why I prepared the way I did, I realize it helped relieve the stress these meetings brought on. If I was very prepared, no one could blindside me. I also knew the importance of starting the year off right and being a good advocate to help my son. I did not want to fail him.

II. Moving away from conflict

We wish that all parent–professional relationships were collaborative. A team approach between parents and professionals is the best model for serving our children with autism. Parents know that they need the expertise of professionals for information, support, and services. Professionals choose to work in this field so they can help meet family needs. And yet, the relationship can become adversarial. Why does the parent's need for help and the professional's desire to help sometimes fail?

A major source of conflict in the parent–professional relationship is the stress inherent in each of these jobs. Both parents and professionals work in an environment of high, if not impossible, demands. Parents and professionals under stress do not lead with their best team-building skills. Working under this kind of pressure makes collaboration difficult and conflicts inevitable. Here are some of the strategies we have used to move from conflict to cooperation.

❈ Lesson 1: Parents bring their own stress to the relationship

There is a saying in the emergency room that, at the time of a crisis, the first pulse you should take is your own. Ultimately, the only parts of our relationship with professionals that we can control are our own actions and reactions. A key to preventing or resolving conflict is to recognize where our stress comes from and how it affects our ability to advocate.

There are many stressors on parents of children with autism that can influence our capacity to advocate for our children. First, there are the physical strains of parenting our children. Many children with autism have sleep difficulties, and, as a result, we are often sleep-deprived. We can become physically exhausted from chasing a hyperactive child around all day. Being in a heightened state of alert all the time can also be physically draining. Parents may choose to ignore their own physical and emotional needs and concentrate more on the needs of the child. This can lead to physical and emotional burnout, something that affects our ability to advocate properly for our child.

Maureen

My first hurdles in learning how to be Justin's advocate were the physical ones. Sleep deprivation and emotional exhaustion interfered with my ability to concentrate. I left many meetings not totally understanding or remembering what was discussed or decided. After one particularly exhausting week, Rob reflected on his switch from the special education teacher to the special education parent side of the relationship. He said, "I never understood why parents looked at me so blankly during our meetings. Now I know."

Especially during the early years following the diagnosis, parents may be overwhelmed with the wide range of emotions. We may be incredibly sad as we adjust to the loss of the child we thought we would have. Many parents feel fear – fear of the future and fear for our child's safety. Understandably, this may make us overly protective of our child. We may feel overwhelmed and confused by the many theories of causes and "cures" and the constant new therapies reported in the media today. Many parents struggle with whether the diagnosis is even correct or which professional to listen to and believe. We may feel guilty and ask ourselves whether we did something wrong or if we should have done something differently. Many parents feel angry. Why did this happen to my child? All these conflicting emotions and the time and energy we must give to the child with autism can make us feel isolated, convinced that no one could possibly understand what we are going through.

We also may feel inadequate as we try to learn about all the services and resources available and how to advocate for our child. Parents of younger children often are frantic, trying to access all the early intervention help they can get for their child. Parents may spend all their time trying to help their child catch up developmentally or worrying about time lost. Even experienced parents at times are unsure of what to do next.

Ann

When Eric was in third grade he was receiving speech and occupational therapies through his IEP. He also had the support of the autism outreach teacher for pull-out time once a week and in the classroom once a week. The learning disabilities (LD) teacher for the school approached me one day and offered to work with Eric once a week. She had met him and liked him and thought she could help him with some of his organizational needs with the academics. I thought it was a great idea. It was such a rare event to have someone come to me to initiate help for Eric.

When I met with the principal about adding LD pull-out time to Eric's IEP, she told me that he was receiving enough services and was being pulled out of class too much as it was. She also said he didn't qualify for LD resource help because he did not have a diagnosis of a learning disability. Following this conversation I talked again to the LD resource teacher and spoke to a "higher-up" in LD services for the school system. I was told that an autism diagnosis would qualify Eric to receive LD resource help.

I met with the principal again to share with her the information I had obtained about LD qualification. She again said that Eric did not need it and that the LD resource teacher was needed for other students. During the conversation I also found out about a previous meeting that had been held with the team about Eric that I was not invited to. When I protested, the principal said in a very condescending tone of voice, "Sometimes, Ms. Palmer, we need to meet without the parent and make decisions."

I was pretty mad and didn't know what to do. Advocating for Eric in the regular education setting was new to me and I wasn't sure of my rights. It was also a new school and I hadn't gotten to know the staff well enough to find an advocate on the campus who could advise me. I found this principal to be very intimidating. I also knew I would need to work with her for several years to come, so I needed to try to keep a good working relationship with her. For this reason I backed down and chose not to pursue the LD pull-out time for Eric. In retrospect, I think I should have done more.

The positive and negative experiences that we have had with professionals in the past can influence our current and future relationships. If our child has been misdiagnosed in the past, if our concerns have been rejected, or we have been judged as "overreactive," it would not be surprising if we felt mistrustful or defensive towards new professionals beginning to work with our child. After spending years dealing with agencies and the schools' bureaucracies, some parents may become burned out and choose to become less involved in advocating for the child. They may have developed a very low tolerance for the inefficiencies of the system after years of struggling with it.

Maureen

As I became comfortable with the role of the advocate, I grew less panicky. However, with experience I also became more easily irritated, and probably more irritating to others. Flexibility is not the defining virtue of large educational and human service systems. As I tried to fit my square-peg child into these round-hole worlds, my tolerance for inflexible systems got extremely low. I grew weary of providing the "Justin 101" lecture for an ever-changing collection of professionals. I was tired of filling out one more form, tired of limited resources hampering the effectiveness of the skilled professionals, and tired of well-intentioned but stupid people. It can be a challenge to keep up the energy and creativity advocates need when they have been doing it for many years. Many situations engender a sense of "here we go again..."

On the other hand, if we have had very positive experiences with professionals in the past, we may have high expectations of future professionals we work with. We may expect more involvement in the therapy or classroom or more communication from the teacher or professional. We may find ourselves disappointed when the new teacher or therapist doesn't live up to our previous experiences.

✳ Lesson 2: Professionals bring their own stress to the relationship

As parents of children with autism we sometimes feel that we have cornered the market on stress. How often do we want to say to other people, "You think *that's* a problem? Let me tell you about problems..." With all the pressures of being a parent, the last thing we may want to consider is the stress of the professionals, especially when they may be causing some of ours! Yet understanding the realities faced by professionals is essential to effective advocacy. Getting our kids what they need requires us to understand the obstacles professional stress can create.

Teachers, physicians, therapists, and caregivers all have stresses that they work with every day. New or inexperienced professionals may have questions about their competency to work with children with autism. For example, regular education teachers often have limited training (if any) in working with children with autism and may feel they do not have the necessary skills. On the other hand, veteran professionals with many years' experience with individuals with autism may become burned out from the cumulative years of working with this population. Their long years of hard work and low pay may make it difficult for these professionals to stay creative or enthusiastic in their work.

Professionals must also deal with the continuing controversy over the causes of autism and appropriate treatments or therapies. There is no standard of practice that is accepted by all. If parents are not happy with the services provided, professionals may have concerns about the possibility of litigation, something that is becoming more and more common in our society. Professionals, especially teachers, may be overwhelmed with the amount of documentation that is required to work with these individuals. They may feel that too much of their time is spent completing paperwork.

In some school systems or direct care programs, the professional may have a lack of administrative support. Professionals often feel underappreciated and underpaid for the work they do. They may feel frustrated by the inadequate level of physical assistance they are given. They can be physically exhausted from their work and feel overwhelmed by the challenge of juggling the needs of many different children. It is also important to remember that the professionals who are serving our children also have personal lives outside of their work that can add to their stress levels. Parents should take into consideration these factors because by appreciating the professional's point of view, parents become better advocates.

Ann

Eric was fully included in regular education classes through most of his school years. Some years were better than others. Eric's first year of inclusion in third grade was one of the hardest. I knew we were in trouble when the notes from the teacher started coming home. The teacher didn't like that Eric's desk was so messy. He obviously was having trouble organizing his books and worksheets and he frequently just threw them into his desk. The teacher also sent a note home complaining that Eric was pacing and talking to himself on the playground during recess. I came to the school and observed him on the playground during recess and he was indeed doing this, but it didn't seem to bother the other children at all. I thought Eric deserved this time during recess to do what relaxed and calmed him since he was holding it together all day in the classroom. Soon after this the teacher sent a note home complaining that Eric was not writing the math problems on the lines correctly. He was getting all the answers correct and he was completing the problems in the time allotted, but she was unhappy because the problems weren't written on the lines.

Obviously the school year was not going as well as I would have liked. One evening the teacher called me at home. I knew it would not be good news. She was calling to suggest to me that because Eric was small for his age, maybe he should be in the second grade instead of third grade. I calmly responded that Eric had already mastered the second-grade curriculum and needed to be in the third grade. I reminded her that in fact he was ahead of third-grade level in reading and math skills. It was obvious to me that she did not want Eric in her class. This was especially frustrating to me because I knew Eric was a good student and well-behaved in her class. He was very rule-bound and would always follow directions in the classroom. I also knew he didn't require much special attention from the teacher, only reminders about turning in work and occasional clarification about the directions for assignments.

I felt that I had done the best job I could as Eric's parent and advocate to educate this teacher about autism and about Eric's strengths and weaknesses. My impression was that this teacher, because of her lack of experience with autism, was scared that Eric might suddenly begin to display the disruptive behaviors of an uncontrollable child with autism. She was not able to see how well Eric was actually doing because she was so worried about what he *might* do.

Over the school year this teacher continued to be overly critical of Eric's differences. A turning point came midway through the year when the teacher called me at home. She had watched a story about autism on a television news program, and the individuals with autism on the show had more serious impairments than Eric. She called me to ask if I had seen the show and then she said, "Eric is really doing quite well, isn't he?" After more than four months she had finally gotten the message that I had been trying to get across to her. Her attitude toward Eric totally changed and from that point on, instead of trying to push him out of her class and not tolerating his differences, she became overly protective of him. She was hesitant to let him try new challenges for fear he would fail. I spent the remainder of the school year advocating for more independent work and challenging experiences for Eric.

To be good advocates for our children, we need to understand not only the constraints on the system and where there may be inadequacies in physical or financial support for the professional, but also the professional's point of view and what level of understanding they have of autism. Not only will this enable us to better understand the professional's position, it will also help us learn where we should focus our advocacy efforts to improve our child's services and the services for other children with autism.

Ann

One thing I learned over the years of advocating for Eric was that professionals often listen better to other professionals than to parents. Maybe they believe other professionals understand their issues better or maybe they think parents can't be as objective because they are too close to the situation. Whatever the reason, I have found that another teacher or member of staff at the school could sometimes make more headway than I could with a problem. The autism outreach teacher was wonderful as a go-between for me and the teachers. If I saw a problem in the class or had a concern, I would talk to the outreach teacher and he would talk to the classroom teacher. I didn't always have to be the complaining parent, possibly straining the relationship between the teacher and me.

Maureen

Conversely, the parent is sometimes in a better position to take the lead in solving a problem than the professional. Justin often needed an aide or additional classroom staff to function well in the classroom. His teachers would recognize the need, but were unable to get the program specialist or their principal to agree and assign additional staff. Because we were parents and not employees, we had tools at our disposal that the teacher did not. Through the IEP process and persistent "diplomacy," we were able to persuade the "powers that be" to assign the additional staff.

※ Lesson 3: Listening is key

Parents and professionals share the same complaint about each other – "They don't listen." This echoes the main complaint in many relationships throughout our culture. We are not a society of great listeners. Listening requires self-control and patience, characteristics that are not always our culture's peak skills. It also requires the precious and scarce commodity of time. But in the long run, taking time to listen saves time.

As parents we bring emotion and passion into situations where we disagree with professionals. We often work very hard to persuade them to agree with the unmistakable merits of our point of view. The problem is that everyone does not see the world the same way we do. So no matter how right we think we are, and how wrong we *know* they are, differences will not be resolved unless we understand their point of view. Listening provides a window into the professional's thinking. By stepping to their side, we understand the obstacles to agreement. Then we can use that information to propose solutions and influence decisions that work for both sides.

Maureen

I developed a relationship with a professional where the only thing we shared was an immediate dislike for each other. I thought she was patronizing and blunt. She thought I was arrogant and defensive. We worked on a committee where we spent more time disagreeing with one another than participating in the work of the committee. One day I was too tired to fall into my usual oppositional monologue in response to her ideas and suggestions. For a change, I gave her my complete attention and listened. What I heard began to change my opinion of her. Hidden behind her way of expressing herself I could hear the real passion and commitment she brought to her work. I discovered that, as an autism teacher, in a system without many resources, she had accomplished remarkable things with her students. I opened up to the possibility that everything she had to contribute might not be as useless as I had assumed.

By listening I opened the door to a new way of relating to her. Over the years, we actually developed a collaborative relationship. She did more to advance my advocacy efforts for Justin than anyone else in the system. I still think she can be patronizing and blunt and she still accuses me of being arrogant and defensive, but we both came to recognize that our negative qualities were not all we had to offer.

✳ Lesson 4: The focus needs to be on interests, not positions

Settling conflicts between parents and professionals requires skill in negotiation. In preparing for a presentation called "Making the Parent–Professional Relationship Work," we found two outstanding books that we wished we had read early on in our advocacy efforts: *Getting to Yes* (Fisher, Ury and Patton 1991) and *Getting Past No* (Ury 1993). Fisher and colleagues define negotiations as "the basic means of getting what you want from others. It is back-and-forth communication designed to reach an agreement when you and the other side have some interests that are shared and others that are opposed" (1991, p.xvii).

The authors say that one reason negotiations fail is that parties get stuck arguing about positions rather than interests. "Positions" are what we decide are our bottom line. "Interests" are what we want to accomplish, and what cause us to make that bottom-line decision. For example, our interest may be that our child develops better language skills. Our position is the child needs individual speech therapy sessions. We may go to an IEP meeting requesting speech therapy sessions five days a week. Our bottom line is three sessions, but we feel that we need to start higher. The school disagrees and thinks that individual speech therapy sessions are not the best model for speech therapy. Besides, they have speech therapist vacancies that they can't fill and a large number of children who require assistance. So their bottom-line position is no. Then each side starts to defend its position, react to the other, respond with nonverbal and verbal displays of frustration, and you know the rest. This produces parents and professionals who not only can't come to an agreement, but who even have trouble sitting down at the table to try. In such a case what is totally missed is any opportunity to discuss the shared *interest*, which is to help the child improve language skills.

Taking time to discuss interests before locking into positions opens up room for creative solutions. There is usually more than one solution to an advocacy issue. In our example, what would have happened if some time was devoted to brainstorming options based on interests? The real-life result was the decision to forgo the daily 15-minute individual therapy sessions with the overscheduled, frazzled speech pathologist. Instead the parents and professionals decided to add the classroom aide in the individual speech therapy sessions that were held once a week and then have the classroom aide work on speech therapy goals with the student throughout each school day. The entire IEP team agreed the solution was the best possible one to meet their shared interests.

❊ Lesson 5: Good communication fosters teamwork

The way that parents communicate with professionals affects our ability to resolve disagreements. Attempting to negotiate while in full "momma bear" mode only makes conflicts worse. No matter how justified we may feel in our anger and frustration, expressing hostility in advocacy settings is ultimately counterproductive. To be an effective advocate requires clear and appropriate communication skills.

(a) Acknowledge their point of view

By listening carefully to the professionals, we gain a clearer understanding of their point of view. We should acknowledge what we have heard before we present our side of the issue. By saying something like "If I understand you correctly, your position is…" we let them know that they have been heard. In the best-case scenario our acknowledgement will make them more receptive to hearing our side. At the very least, we have modeled the attention and respect that we expect in return. Acknowledging the professionals' point of view is not the same as agreeing. It is also not caving in. We can be absolutely opposed to what they have to say. But if we do not make them feel that we understand where they are coming from, we risk spending the entire meeting talking past each other.

(b) Agree where you can

Before we present how we differ from the professional's point of view, we should first try to accentuate the areas where we agree. By recognizing that we share common ground, we create an atmosphere where collaboration and team problem-solving is possible. We increase the confidence of both sides that we can solve a particular conflict because we already have so many issues that we agree upon.

(c) Say "and," not "but"

This communication skill will not only help with professionals, it will also help communication with our spouse and our teenagers. Once people hear "but" in a sentence they tend not to listen. Feeling contradicted, they erase the areas of agreement and focus on the areas where they disagree. Using "and" allows you to add to the discussion without the implied criticism of "but;" for example, "Yes, we have made considerable progress in getting Justin out into the community, and I believe we can improve even more by adding an afternoon to the schedule."

(d) Make "I" statements

In describing our point of view, we should speak from the place where we have the most expertise – our own experience. Using "I" statements like "I feel..." and "I am frustrated..." makes people less defensive than statements that start with "you." "I" statements describe how the present situation affects us. It tells the professionals what *we* need, rather than attacking them for what *they* are not doing for us. Keeping our remarks in the first person can reduce the defensiveness of the professionals and help them be more receptive to our point of view. The less energy each side uses in defending its position, the more energy there is for focusing on solving the problems.

Maureen

I was once locked in a battle with professionals over school transportation. After living an absurd comedy of errors for several weeks, my approach became a demanding, accusing litany of "You people..." The result of my approach was that the situation got even worse. On top of the problem of no transportation, now no one returned any of my calls. Finally I spoke to someone who met my hostility with her own. Totally exasperated, I said, "I am so frustrated by this situation. I don't know what to do next. I have a severely disabled child, a toddler, and a newborn. I have not slept in weeks. If I can't figure out how to get this problem solved, I will need to hide the sharp implements. I really need the bus to show up. What would you do if you were in my position?"

Well, it turned out she *was* in my position, at least enough to understand. She also had school-age kids, a toddler, and newborn. She knew what it was like to be sleep-deprived and crazed. By avoiding "you" statements, I lowered her defensiveness. By using "I" statements, I opened some room for her to identify and empathize with me. She told me she would take care of the problem and she did. I wrote this transportation supervisor a thank-you note and dropped off some flowers as well. I was ready to give her the deed to my house for fixing our problem with bus transportation. She remained the person I called at the first sign of school transportation trouble. As parents who use special transportation services know, that meant I got to speak with her at least several times during the year.

This experience taught me two additional lessons about advocacy. When you find a person who is receptive and able to help you navigate the school or human services system, keep them close. Gatekeepers like this woman are an invaluable resource. Make them your new best friends. Sometimes gatekeepers can be found in places you do not expect. The custodial and cafeteria staffs at schools, along with the school secretaries, have been some of the most helpful school staff I have encountered.

The other lesson I learned from the experience is that asking for advice can be more effective than making demands. Sometimes I feel like I am being manipulative when I ask for advice, and to some extent I probably am. I have learned that there are professionals who will get on my side if I massage their egos and ask for their expertise. I use that knowledge to my advantage when making requests; but my asking advice is also a genuine request for ideas and information. It has yielded far better advocacy results for Justin than when I have marched into a professional's office with my list of demands.

✳ Lesson 6: Emotions need to be removed from the conflict

The hardest strategy to use in resolving our conflicts with professionals is refusing to react. After all, we are at our most emotional when we are discussing the needs of our child. The passion and emotion that we bring to our advocacy makes it almost impossible not to respond when we feel we are being dismissed, patronized, or attacked. When we believe our children are not getting what they need, our instinctive response is to fight. The prevailing wisdom of many parents supports this approach as the most effective way to get what you need. Parents go into disagreements armed for a fight, guns blazing. It is no longer the squeaky wheel that gets the most attention. It's the wheel that rolls over and crushes the other side. This approach has the added advantage of making us feel more powerful and in control. But while we may end up getting back or getting even, we do not get what we want (Ury 1993).

From our experience, this "take no prisoners" approach with professionals does not work. Over the long term, when we react emotionally in a conflict with professionals, we lose the focus on our child. "Speak when you are angry and you make the best speech you will ever regret" (Ury 1993, p.31). We give the professionals the justification for their belief that parents are demanding and hostile. Rather than focusing on reaching agreement, our collaboration degenerates into a futile chain reaction of accusations and counteraccusations. We damage a relationship that in the long run is more important than the particular conflict.

Invariably, the person we anger the most will go on to a position of authority, where they will become an even bigger obstacle in our path. Even if we win in the short term, do we really want people who are angry with us to be the caregivers or teachers for our children with autism? Enlightened self-interest requires us to pursue other ways to resolve our conflicts. Here are some ways to fight the temptation to react.

(a) Do an attitude check

Our attitudes can create self-fulfilling prophecies. If we go into meetings with the view that professionals are the enemy, we will have done our part to make them act like they are. "Put on your radar, not your armor" (Ury 1993, p.43) is advice worth taking. Assume intelligence and good intentions until proven otherwise.

(b) Don't go into meetings with a professional when you are angry

The likelihood of resolving differences is very low when you start from a hostile position. Find a friend or another professional to listen. Rant, scream, cuss, cry, and stamp as long and as hard as it takes to calm down. Releasing the tension beforehand helps prevent us from blowing our tops in the meeting.

(c) Understand your hot buttons

Our bodies often provide the first signs that someone is pushing our buttons; we start to feel the rapid pulse, the sweaty palms, and the tightly set jaw. It is important we recognize the signs early, before we act on our uncontrollable urge to leap over the table and choke someone. The author of *Getting Past No* offers a suggestion for when we start to react:

> When you find yourself facing a difficult negotiation, you need to step back, collect your wits, and see the situation objectively. Imagine you are negotiating on a stage and then imagine yourself climbing onto a balcony looking over the stage. The "balcony" is a metaphor for a mental attitude of detachment. From the balcony you can calmly evaluate the conflict almost as if you were a third party. (Ury 1993, p.38)

If all else fails we found another effective strategy is to bring someone with us who knows when to kick us under the table.

Maureen

My number one hot button has always been what I call "the triple whammy." The first step is setting Justin up to fail, usually by not listening to my suggestions or dismissing my advice as the ravings of an overprotective parent. The second step is letting him fail, which sometimes involved someone getting hurt. The third step is blaming him by making him the bad guy and the cause of the problem. For example, at the beginning of high school I repeatedly suggested to anyone who would listen that Justin required a harness seat belt to stay in his seat on the bus. Several weeks later, the bus ran very late and Justin got out of his seat and hit the bus driver on top of his head. I received a call from the person at school transportation who was responsible for getting the seat belts in the first place (she was also the person who never returned my calls). She announced in a most patronizing voice that Justin was suspended from the bus because he "assaulted" the bus driver. If I could have come through the phone, I would have strangled her. What I wanted to scream was, "And you wonder why parents are hostile!?!"

It took a lot of work to get myself to calm down. I called friends and some trusted professionals and vented my head off. Once I calmed down, I worked with the reasonable professionals in the system to get the seat belt, a transfer to a different bus and bus driver, and a transportation supervisor who was prepared to be more accommodating. Fortunately, the woman who kicked Justin off the bus (which exceeded her authority in the first place) did not cross my path again.

(d) Use silence

Sometimes saying nothing at all to an attack or a stupid remark can defuse a situation. First of all, it allows you time to take a deep breath and try to remove the emotion from your response. It allows you to say to yourself "Is this person an idiot or what?" *before* you blurt it out loud to the group. It also provides time for the professional (a.k.a., the idiot who may have overstated the last remark) to reconsider and modify what he or she just said. It almost always makes someone in the meeting uncomfortable and perhaps willing to offer some middle-ground position.

(e) Remember that staying cool, calm, and collected can be its own reward

Maureen

I learned a lesson about refusing to react from my son Michael. While playing high-school basketball, he never got involved in trash talk with opposing players. I asked him how he kept his cool when he was being taunted. He told me that your opponent wants you to talk back so you will lose your focus. If you do not respond, you can concentrate better on the ball and the direction it is going. Then, with a devilish look in his eye, he added, "Besides, when you don't respond it drives the other guy crazy." That may be the guilty pleasure we can derive from refusing to react.

✳ Lesson 7: Use persistence to your advantage

Parents may not have power or money on their side, but persistence can be our secret weapon. One of the lessons our children have taught us is the power of not giving up. How many times have we given in to our kids because their persistence wore us down? By applying the same principle we can sometimes get the concessions we want. Parents can use the "broken record" approach (we are dating ourselves with that reference!). Repeat the same message in cool, calm, and collected ways. Hostility will negate the effects of persistence. Our approach needs to be subtle, almost subliminal, to be really effective (and sufficiently annoying). Eventually it will become apparent that we are not giving up or going away. Someone will often act on our behalf if only to move the needle off the broken record.

Maureen

When Justin was in middle school, his autism classroom went through a parade of unqualified teachers. The principal of the school was a nice enough guy, but he was clueless in how to recruit and hire for the position. He basically hired anyone with a pulse who walked through his door.

My friend Chris and I were determined that the teacher turnover had to stop. We decided to look for a qualified teacher ourselves. While we started to network to find possible candidates, I noticed a new teacher assistant at Michael's and Patrick's elementary school. Kevin had accepted a temporary job as a one-to-one aide for a child with severe behavioral difficulties. He was in the final days of school to get his Master's degree and was in the market for a full-time middle-school teaching position. Once I observed that he was an exceptionally skilled and compassionate teacher, Chris and I got in touch with the principal. With a sense of great urgency we encouraged the principal to act right away. A week later, he had still not interviewed Kevin.

While he delayed, the substitute teacher in the classroom was starting to unravel. We sort of figured that the fact that she was in tears at the end of each school day was not a good sign. Like canaries in the coal mine, we had sensed the first signals that she would not be with us much longer. So Chris and I decided to use the broken record approach. Every day one of us would call the principal or stop by his office to chat about whether he had had a chance to interview Kevin. Doing our best "Stepford Wives" imitation, we tried to keep our exasperation with his inaction under wraps. We knew from experience that when he became defensive, it became even harder to get anything accomplished. We calmly kept up the pressure until he got tired and moved the needle. He finally interviewed Kevin and offered him the job. All our effort paid off, as Kevin was one of the best teachers Justin ever had.

Ann

I called the housing office on campus as the first step towards obtaining a private dormitory room for Eric. A nice woman answered the phone. I told her that I was inquiring about getting a private dorm room for my son who has autism. (I already knew two students on the autism spectrum who had received this accommodation at this university.) She promptly said, "You can't have a single dorm room unless you have asthma or some medical condition like that." It was immediately obvious to me that I was not talking to the right person to help me and I asked to talk to her supervisor. Sometimes as we advocate for our children, we need to make sure the person we are talking to has the right information and is empowered to make decisions.

✳ Lesson 8: You may have to defend your child's need for services

Some of our children on the autism spectrum are able to be included in regular education programs, either full-time or part-time. While this can be a wonderful achievement, it also can complicate our advocacy responsibilities. We often have to advocate for our child to initially receive services and frequently have to fight for the services to continue long term. If the student is successful academically, which many of our high-functioning or Asperger students are, the school may assume the student doesn't need supports and may want to withdraw services. In reality the student may be performing well academically *because* of the supports he or she receives. But he or she also may be struggling with non-academic issues such as social or organizational problems in school.

If the student has a diagnosis of an autism spectrum disorder (ASD), it can help in accessing services. Many parents have concerns about their child receiving the label of autism in school. We may be worried that the label will somehow limit the opportunities for our child. Perhaps teachers won't challenge the student to reach full potential if they know the child has an ASD. Maybe they will treat the child differently. We want our children to blend with their peers and compete on a fair playing field. However, most of our children do not totally blend and frequently have behaviors that set them apart. A diagnosis of ASD in school can supply an explanation for the student's differences when they arise. The diagnosis can help the student to qualify initially for services from the school and can also serve as a way to defend the ongoing need for supports when the student is doing well and the school questions whether supports are necessary.

Many of these students who can be mainstreamed or included in regular education do not have obvious needs unless time is spent getting to know them. They may not fit neatly into a self-contained classroom model for children with autism and they may not fit neatly into the regular education classroom setting. These are the kids who can fall through the cracks, and parents and school personnel must be creative in determining appropriate placement for these students. We may have to advocate for something that the school does not typically do. We may need to remind ourselves that IEP stands for *Individualized* Education Plan.

Ann

Frequently over the years of Eric's schooling I needed to defend his need for supports. It usually happened at the beginning of a new school year when the teacher would see that Eric's grades from the previous year were good and assume he was doing fine and didn't need the extra help I was trying to arrange for him. I would then need to explain that his grades were good *because* of the extra organizational help he was given. Someone once told me the perfect example I could share with a teacher in this situation: Would you take away the glasses from a student because he or she was seeing well?

III. Realizing that sometimes advocacy fails

Despite all our best advocacy skills, sometimes we run up against situations that we can't fix. It forces us to face the reality that some problems resist resolution and that sometimes our choice becomes finding the least objectionable alternative. Times like these are extremely difficult because there are no easy answers for what to do next. Here are the survival lessons we have learned.

❊ Lesson 1: Parents may need to reach out to their support systems

Intractable disagreements with professionals can deplete all our energy and make us feel lost and alone. When we come up against situations that we can't repair, our first inclination may be to isolate ourselves. Moving towards the people who can support us offers a better alternative. Sometimes someone just "hearing us out" can reveal new options to consider.

Maureen

Justin's behavior in high school was extremely difficult to manage. It was caused by a combustible mixture of his anxious adolescence and an insecure and disorganized teacher. From my perspective, Justin was continually being set up to fail. Our county school system assembled a group of behavioral experts to try to devise a plan of action. Despite having what I knew were really good intentions, we were still just paving the road to hell. The teacher called me daily to pick up Justin from class. While I knew this was not resolving the problem, I could not leave him in a class where he was hurting himself and potentially someone else.

I had gone through the usual litany of emotions: panic, frustration, anger, sadness, and now depression, because for one of the first times in Justin's life, I could see no way out of this mess. I had done all the things I advised others to do and my advocacy was a complete failure. I was in the middle of this no-win situation when I met with the school psychologist for Justin's psychological re-evaluation. By the time I got to the appointment with the psychologist, I had no energy for the present and no vision of the future. By the time I left, I felt as if the weight of the world had been lifted off my shoulders.

On my way home, I tried to figure out why I felt better. We had not solved a thing. We had not devised a new plan. There was nothing specific that had been accomplished. Then I realized what I felt was the therapeutic power of being heard and acknowledged. The psychologist said very little and when she spoke it was to encourage me to continue. She allowed me to vent and get all the past injustices and failures off my chest without being defensive. She apologized by saying she was sorry for what I had been through, without blaming her colleagues or even agreeing with me. She said, "I am sorry. You and Justin do not deserve to be having such a difficult time." I thought to myself "Has any professional ever apologized to me before? Do they know what a powerful gift an apology can be?"

Before I left, the psychologist assured me that while we had not yet found the answers, the team would not give up trying. That conversation provided an incredible release of the emotional energy I was expending just running in place. During the following week I found new energy and perspective to take a new look at the situation. I recognized that we needed a totally different approach to Justin's educational program. Rob and I decided that Justin was getting out of the classroom.

✳ Lesson 2: Sometimes you have to get out if you can

When all our advocacy efforts fail, we need time to consider our options. In some situations it may be time to cut our losses and get out. We have had friends pursue many different paths for getting out of a no-win situation and into something better, from moving within the system to moving outside it. Some have removed their children from public school for schooling at home or transferred them to private education programs. Some have changed from private programs back to the public schools. Others have moved to another community to access more appropriate services. All these decisions carried significant financial and emotional costs for these families. Before severing ties with present services, it was crucial for them to have a circle of trusted advisors for advice and support.

Maureen

Once we decided that Justin would not be returning to high school, we looked at the options we had. We were fortunate to have a residential and vocational farm program for people with autism in a community 45 minutes away. The director of the farm was one of the advisors I had consulted about Justin over the years. She offered Justin the opportunity to work at the farm, with a job coach. We accepted.

But I was still bothered by our unsuccessful attempts to get Justin's needs met within the public-school system. The team we assembled failed to develop the programs for children like Justin whose behavioral needs interfered with their ability to reach their vocational goals. I decided that since Justin was entitled to three more years of public education, I would try to influence the school system to support this different approach. Planning long and hard over how I could make it easy for the school system to do the right thing, I met with the autism program specialist.

And who was the person who could convince the system to do this? It was the professional on the committee whom I had initially disliked and discounted! Fortunately, by now we had developed a high level of trust. I basically said, "I know you have tried to bring all the services you can think of to bear on this problem, yet it still is untenable. I have tried my best to be a team player. Because of his behavior, none of Justin's vocational and community goals have been met. You know I could use legal recourse, but that will get us nowhere. We need a new approach." I explained I had found the place and the program. Justin already had a one-to-one aide who wanted to get out of the classroom as well. All the school system needed to do was assign the aide and pay for transportation. This professional advocated on my behalf and the school system reluctantly agreed. For the last three years of high school Justin worked on the farm four days a week and attended the high school one day a week.

✳ Lesson 3: Sometimes all you can do is make the best of a bad situation

Sometimes we don't have the luxury of getting out of a bad situation. At least temporarily, all we might be able to do is to minimize the damage wherever we can. We can try to supplement what our child is not getting in their program by using outside resources. At the same time, we can work with an advocacy group or other dissatisfied parents to effect the improvements where they need to be made.

If the advocacy impasse is at school, finding additional classroom help with an experienced aide can sometimes offset the deficits of an unqualified teacher. So can arranging for time out of the classroom with a more sympathetic or competent member of the school staff. This is where our knowledge of school personnel comes in handy. The staff member who can provide a safe haven for our child might be found in a variety of places.

Maureen

Justin spent three of his elementary school years in a segregated special education school. There were several excellent autism teachers who were tireless advocates for their students. During Justin's last year at the school, his teacher was decidedly *not* one of those teachers.

His teacher had a resumé that looked great on paper with all the best training possible. But in reality, her abilities were a terrible fit with Justin's needs. Justin's behavior grew worse in her classroom. We brought in outside consultation to no avail. I recognized that the classroom situation was not going to be resolvable and we needed a change of personnel.

We were six months away from a move to a different city. Having observed at the new school, I knew that it would be a vast improvement. What I needed was a short-term solution, and I considered the options I saw in the school.

I could not expect much help from the school administration. The school was originally developed for children with physical disabilities and had only recently inherited the autism classes. This was not a popular inheritance for a significant number of the school's personnel. The school's culture was based on a caste system where the children with autism were clearly in the "untouchables" category.

So I turned my attention to how I could minimize Justin's time with this current teacher. I had one ally in the classroom, an aide who had more compassion and common sense than the rest of the classroom staff combined. I knew for the time she was with him each morning, he would at least receive safe and compassionate care. I was left to find someone to work with Justin and someplace to go each afternoon. The best autism teachers had no room in their classrooms. Then I had an epiphany. Justin loved to swim and the school had an indoor pool. I was a lifeguard and frequently volunteered at the pool. I knew the physical education teachers in charge of the pool were both skilled and compassionate people. We arranged for Justin to swim during the day whenever he needed a break from the classroom.

In those six months, the only skill Justin learned was to improve his ability to swim. But changing the people who worked with him during the day diminished a lot of his disruptive behaviors. I felt like we did the best that we could given the choices we had.

There are few consolations we can offer when you feel locked into services that are not meeting the needs of your child. In the world of school services, parents have due process rights and can pursue a grievance procedure all the way up to a lawsuit. Whether to pursue legal recourse is a difficult question which only the parents involved can decide. Consulting with your circle of trusted professionals and parent advisors, as well as an advocacy organization, can be helpful in making that decision.

The only consolation we can provide from personal experiences is that in no-win situations, our children were often more resilient than we were. We believed that those bad situations would ruin the rest of their lives. We worried about losing time that we would never get back. But, as we learned, our children had a greater capacity to recover from negative situations than we had realized.

IV. Recognizing "best practice" qualities of professionals

Through trial and error, through good relationships and bad, we have a clearer understanding now of what qualities we would look for in a professional with whom we want to work.

Ann

One professional who made a huge difference in both my life and Maureen's life was Dr. Lee Marcus, the director of the Chapel Hill TEACCH Center. He led a mothers' support group that we both attended. Despite being the only male in the room, and the only person who was not a parent of a child with autism, we easily accepted him as "one of us." Dr. Marcus had this wonderful way of making the mothers feel comfortable and safe, and in his quiet, nonjudgmental way, he listened to us. Even though he was the Ph.D. in the room and had more years of experience and knowledge about autism than we all had put together, we knew he was learning from us.

There are many reasons why this particular parent–professional relationship was so easy and helpful. It was an effortless relationship to develop because from day one he made us feel like we were the experts and that what we had to say was important. We knew he respected us because after years of working with families, he understood the difficulties we were facing with our children. He also never judged us when we got a little carried away with our anger towards a particular teacher or when we were unrealistic about our expectations for our children. We could be open and honest with our feelings because we knew we could trust him.

This parent–professional relationship was also beneficial because Dr. Marcus facilitated, rather than telling us what to do. He helped us reach our own conclusions and our own decisions by allowing us to talk things through with each other. But when we needed his expertise about autism or about treatments or behavior strategies, he was honest and didn't avoid the difficult questions. If he didn't have the information we needed he would help us find it.

It amazes me to think how well he handled this volatile group of overly emotional, frustrated, confused, and scared mothers. The real testament to what this relationship meant to all of us is how it has survived over time. The mothers from this original support group that gathered almost 20 years ago still reach out to Dr. Marcus for support and advice as our once-young children are now entering adulthood. Even though we don't meet with him on a regular basis anymore, the mutual respect and trust still exist.

✳ They listened

The most important relationship-building strategy both parents and professionals can use is to listen. The best professionals we worked with listened and acknowledged our point of view, even when they did not agree. Being heard and understood was a powerful release for our stress. Listening was the first step toward gaining our trust.

These professionals recognized that understanding the parent's point of view enhances the ability to work as a team. They got to know us and stepped into our world. They put our behavior into context. For example, they did not dismiss us as overprotective, but listened and used our suggestions to make their work with our children more effective. They understood our schedule conflicts and changed meetings to accommodate us, rather than complaining that parents do not participate. They recognized the levels of stress in our families and gave us "homework" that fit into the realities of our family life.

Maureen

During a year when juggling the needs of Justin, a toddler, and a newborn resulted in a lot of dropped balls, I approached reading the Parent Progress Report from Justin's school with a sense of dread. In the section called "Recommendations for Home," the teacher wrote, "I really haven't any recommendations to make other than keep up the good job you are already doing with him." There is a special place in heaven for teachers like that.

These professionals encouraged us to tell them our stories. Understanding our history with other professionals, they did not take our occasional "momma bear" responses as personal attacks. Without getting defensive, they allowed us to let off steam relating our past grievances and frustrations in getting services for our child. Being able to express our frustrations with the system helped us move on from a focus on past injustices to the work we needed to do in the present.

❊ They saw our children, not just the diagnosis

More than anyone else in our lives after autism, professionals have been in the position to see our children and not just a diagnosis. That ability helped us feel less alone. As new parents, it was easy for us to focus on our children's delays and deficits. The best professionals provided a counterbalance by helping us to see our children's strengths.

Maureen

When Justin was three, I remember filling out an interview form for autism preschool. When I came to the section that asked me to list Justin's strengths, I started to cry. I could not think of any. I was so overwhelmed by the negatives of autism that I needed help appreciating the positives in my child. The report from Justin's evaluation provided my first lesson in advocacy. Everyone is a mixture of weaknesses and strengths. Lead with your strengths.

The report read: "The following behavioral strengths and weaknesses were noted in Justin: affectionate, interacts with adults, self-feeds with utensils, good eye contact, occupies himself in play, sense of humor…" Just the placement of the strengths before the weaknesses made it easier to read the rest of the paragraph: "…significant language delay, not toilet trained, mouths objects, eats non-edibles, aggressive, unable to communicate appropriately, limited attending skills." My usual reaction to reading Justin's evaluations was to obsess about all of his weaknesses. This time I was too intrigued that someone believed my nonverbal son had a sense of humor to obsess about his weaknesses. It turned out to be a prophetic report. As the years passed, I came to believe that a sense of humor is one of Justin's most endearing qualities.

Ann

Eric had been going to an occupational therapist for several years. She was great with him and understood how to use his strengths to help address his weaknesses. On her own initiative, she worked on social and communication issues while focusing on the fine and gross motor problems that were her expertise. I trusted her and respected her opinion. One day she very nicely said to me, "You know, Eric could be potty trained now. I think you need to start." I had not started potty training him at all, partly because I was dreading it and partly because I didn't know he was ready. I was so immersed in Eric's autism and his therapies that I had lost sight of the "typical" developmental issues of a toddler. She probably struggled with whether she should say anything to me because I could have taken it as a criticism of my parenting skills. Of course, it turned out she was right. I started potty training Eric and he caught on almost immediately. I appreciated this therapist pointing out something to me about my son that I couldn't see.

Sometimes professionals can be quite creative in putting a positive spin on our children's behavior. They help us find some perspective and humor.

Maureen

My favorite spin on Justin's behavior came during his legendary biting stage, with a classroom aide as his favorite target. Justin had a great teacher who knew that I somehow felt responsible. She managed the difficult task of giving me honest reports about his day, without making me feel worse than I already did. She was the first teacher who taught me that Justin's behavior was communicative. She always put his behavior in the context of what he was trying to tell us. One day I got a short note in his communication book that read:

> I think Justin was tired today because he had a difficult afternoon. He bit Sally [the classroom aide] several times... He's always been such a good judge of character. I doubt she will be with us much longer.

When Sally was fired the next week, I learned that no one in the school had been impressed by her compassion or her expertise. They felt Justin had acted on their behalf.

✳ They believed in us

Because we felt inadequate as new parents, it was easy to dwell on our parental flaws and failures. Professionals helped us see our strengths. When we felt better about our ability as parents, it increased our confidence and self-esteem. We lost some of our anxiety and found more energy to tackle the problems we faced.

Ann

One of the most positive relationships I have had with a professional was with the autism outreach teacher from my son's school system. This person came into our lives when Eric was entering fourth grade and he continued supporting Eric throughout his school career until his graduation from high school. Over the nine years he worked with Eric, he not only helped Eric survive and prosper in school, he also helped me in many ways as well. He was someone I could go to when I was worried about Eric, when I had questions about autism, or when I needed advice about advocacy. If there was a problem with a particular class, I could call him and we would talk it through and come up with a plan to help Eric. Sometimes because of the constraints on the system we had to be creative and he was always willing to think outside the box.

When I look back over the years of his work with Eric and me, I have tried to determine what it was about this particular working relationship that made it so successful. It was obvious to me that he believed in his job and cared about Eric and the many other students he was helping. He also respected the knowledge parents have about their children and considered that information crucial in understanding students and learning how to help them. He never made me feel that my concerns were unfounded or trivial. He was also honest enough with me that he could give me a reality check now and then if I needed it. I occasionally needed him to remind me of aspects of Eric's autism that I would lose sight of, or to remind me that Eric was ready for a challenge that I was afraid to pursue. Our communications were open and easy and everything felt less threatening and more attainable after our conversations.

This was a parent–professional relationship that was based on mutual respect and good communication. I tried not to expect more from him than he could give and reminded him frequently that I was supportive of what he did and appreciated his efforts for my child. In return, he always treated me as an equal partner on the team and valued my opinions. As the years went by, Eric needed his support in the classroom less and less, which is how it should be. As I became more knowledgeable about Eric and a stronger advocate for him within the school, I also became less dependent on the outreach teacher's support. He helped us both become more independent and more confident, something that we will always be grateful for.

✳ They respected parent–professional boundaries

Working closely together, it is easy for parents and professionals to become friends. After all, each group is so remarkably likeable! However, there is potential for problems when parents and professionals change a collaborative professional relationship into a personal one. The first problem is the temptation to reveal too much personal information. Nothing erodes trust faster than breaking a confidence or speaking negatively to a parent about another student or parent. This sounds so basic, yet over the years we have seen professionals violate confidentiality policies far too often. When professionals have crossed that line with us, we always wonder what is being said about us behind our backs. The best professionals always kept confidential information and negative comments to themselves and thereby earned our trust.

Another danger is that friendships can complicate the relationship when differences arise. It is highly unlikely that parents and professionals will be in agreement on every issue concerning the child with autism. Resolving differences between a parent and professional who have developed a friendship gets incredibly messy. Feelings of betrayal or ill will can make further collaboration impossible. Having made this mistake several times, we learned to wait until our children were no longer under their professional's care to pursue a personal relationship.

❋ They connected us with resources

When our needs exceeded their capacity to help, the best professionals enlarged our circle of support by connecting us to additional resources. One of the best resources was other parents, especially when their children were similar to ours. If we were hesitant to take the first step, the professionals offered to sit in on a first introduction or attend a group meeting with us. One teacher, who felt the new parents in her class needed support but were hesitant to reach out for it, organized a monthly brown-bag lunch in her classroom with speakers and discussions about topics of interest.

Advocating for our children is obviously much more than attending meetings and signing IEP forms. We have discussed how to build a positive parent–professional relationship and how to foster cooperation and manage conflict. In the next chapter we will discuss the importance of taking care of ourselves so that we can be the most effective advocates for our children.

Lessons for advocating for our children

I. Building positive relationships with professionals

1. Decide what you want for your child.

2. Children should participate in advocacy as they are able.

3. Parents need to develop advocacy skills:

   (a) Meet the teacher and other professionals before the program begins

   (b) Share information about your child

   (c) Be an ambassador for your child

   (d) Provide the "Autism 101" on your child

   (e) Get to know the professional

   (f) Pick your battles

   (g) Share information about issues that may be affecting your child

   (h) Offer to help

   (i) Offer moral support.

4. It helps to get organized.

II. Moving away from conflict

1. Parents bring their own stress to the relationship.

2. Professionals bring their own stress to the relationship.

3. Listening is key.

4. The focus needs to be on interests, not positions.

5. Good communication fosters teamwork:

   (a) Acknowledge their point of view

(b) Agree where you can

(c) Say "and," not "but"

(d) Make "I" statements.

6. Emotions need to be removed from the conflict:

(a) Do an attitude check

(b) Don't go into meetings with a professional when you are angry

(c) Understand your hot buttons

(d) Use silence

(e) Remember that staying cool, calm, and collected can be its own reward.

7. Use persistence to your advantage.

8. You may have to defend your child's need for services.

III. Realizing that sometimes advocacy fails

1. Parents may need to reach out to their support systems.

2. Sometimes you have to get out if you can.

3. Sometimes all you can do is make the best of a bad situation.

IV. Recognizing "best practice" qualities of professionals

- They listened.

- They saw our children, not just the diagnosis.

- They believed in us.

- They respected parent–professional boundaries.

- They connected us with resources.

Chapter 6

Taking Care of Ourselves

Failing to take care of ourselves is an occupational hazard of mother-hood. While we know that we need time for self-care, it is often the first thing mothers sacrifice at the altar of their families. Anne Morrow Lindbergh described this challenge of motherhood:

> It is basically: how to remain whole in the midst of the distractions of life; how to remain balanced, no matter what centrifugal forces tend to pull one off center; how to remain strong, no matter what shocks come in at the periphery and tend to crack the hub of the wheel. (Lindbergh 1955, p.29)

We believe that autism qualifies as a distracting, unbalancing, wheel-cracking centrifugal force, all on its own. As such, it threatens to con-sume all of our time and energy. In an attempt to meet the needs of others, we move our own needs to the bottom of the priority list. This creates sleep-deprived, irritable, burned-out mothers who help neither themselves nor their children.

Raising a child with autism is a marathon, not a sprint. To finish this race, it is essential to pace ourselves and find ways to create, conserve, and restore our physical and emotional energy. When our lives leave us exhausted, we can catch our breath by taking some advice from the air-lines: In the event of a loss of cabin pressure, place the oxygen mask on yourself first, and then help your child. What follows are some lessons we've learned about taking care of ourselves.

❋ Lesson 1: Sleep is a priority

Lack of sleep drains our energy and affects our ability to cope. Fatigue robs us of perspective and the capacity to focus, concentrate, and solve problems. By increasing levels of the stress hormone cortisol, sleep deprivation wreaks havoc with our emotions. It can make us feel hopeless, irritable, angry, and depressed. How many conflicts with family members or autism professionals are caused by exhaustion? No wonder sleep deprivation is used in psychological warfare as an effective form of torture.

To take care of ourselves, we must be relentless in making sleep a priority. When your child has a disturbance in sleep, it is crucial to find people and resources to help solve the problem. In the meantime, sleep while your child is asleep or at school, even when that requires that other tasks go undone. Consider a sitter or perhaps a family member to periodically "work the night shift" at your house. Ask teachers and care providers to increase the amount of physical activity your child has during the day. Ask them not to let your child nap at school. Talk to your child's doctor regarding the use of sleep medication. Be aware that children with autism sometimes have paradoxical reactions, so some sleep medications can have the opposite effect. You may need to try several different kinds.

Ann

I took naps. When Eric and the baby slept, I slept. Sometimes I just lay down and closed my eyes and rested, forcing myself not to worry about the laundry or the messy house. The brief time sleeping or resting rejuvenated me for what was left of my day. Taking baths was also a relaxing escape for me. If my husband was home and available to take care of the kids, I would make a hot bubble bath and sit and soak while reading a book. If necessary, I would lock the door to guarantee privacy and a short time of uninterrupted relaxation.

Maureen

I also used locks, but not in the same way that Ann did. Most nights I was hypersensitive to noise from the kids and would get out of bed if I heard even a peep. Occasionally, however, Justin would wake up while we were asleep and quietly get out of his room. At minimum, he would entertain himself for the night by rearranging the house, especially the food from the kitchen shelves and the fridge. At worst, he consumed a bottle of medication, despite my best efforts to childproof our house. We decided to install a lock on the outside of his bedroom door, one that was easy to open in case of emergency. I had visions of a social worker charging me with child abuse and neglect for locking my child in his room. But after Justin consumed the bottle of medicine, I decided the lock on his door was the only way to keep him safe during the night.

Justin was usually out for the night once he fell asleep. It was getting to sleep that could be problematic. Over time, he would fall asleep later and later at night. Left to his own devices, he would totally reverse his days and nights. I initially resisted the notion of sleep medication. After staying up late with Justin one too many nights in a row, I decided that medication was preferable to opening the bedroom window and pushing him out (or jumping out myself!). We used medication when Justin began the cycle of reversing his days and nights. It took one or two nights of a drug-induced bedtime before he resumed a normal pattern of sleep.

Sometimes the culprit robbing our sleep is not our child.

Maureen

Sometimes I was my own worst enemy at getting the sleep I needed. I savored the time at night when everyone was finally asleep and I could have the house to myself. I wanted the time to sit down with a glass of wine and relax with a book or the TV. The next day I would discover the truth of the Law of Diminishing Returns. Getting anything done in my state of fatigue took so much longer than it did when I was well rested. The quality of what I was trying to accomplish would suffer. I compromised with my competing needs by going to sleep when Justin did, at least most of the nights of the week. I consoled myself with the increasing evidence that sleep can decrease your body mass index. Losing weight by simply going to sleep gave me another compelling reason to go to bed when Justin did.

Sometimes my sleep was interrupted by fear and anxiety. I could not stop my mind from spinning over my present troubles and frightening scenarios of the future. On nights like these, I found two activities that helped me to clear my head and allow me to get back to sleep. The first was to write a fast and furious stream of consciousness list of all the things that were troubling me. Julia Cameron says, "Writing 'rights' things," and often that proved to be true (Cameron 1998, p.17). (One problem with this practice is that I now have many journals stashed in my closet documenting the hard times of my adult life. I've told Rob that if he reads my journals after I am gone, to remember that I was not nearly as suicidal and homicidal as the journals might lead him to believe.) The second antidote to insomnia was getting out of bed and losing myself in some routine activity like washing the dishes or cleaning the house. Being productive at least provided me some small compensation for losing sleep.

❋ Lesson 2: We can allow ourselves to be a "good enough" parent

On top of the time-consuming demands of raising our children, we add personal and cultural pressure to be an all-competent mom. In a terrific article in *Newsweek* titled "The Good Enough Mother," Anna Quindlen cautions against the epidemic of "manic motherhood" (Quindlen 2005, p.50). Mothers go to extremes in the pursuit of every activity that might help their children both stand out and fit in. We torment ourselves in the pursuit of being the perfect mom.

Maureen

During Michael's and Patrick's elementary school years, I felt that I needed to volunteer for all their activities in school. When Patrick was in fifth grade, I was asked to bring several platters of peanut butter and jelly sandwiches to school for a party. The request was followed by instructions to cut the sandwiches in the shape of a star. Given our chaotic life at home, I did not start my star-making adventure until late that night. Since accessorizing food is not one of my strengths, my sandwiches made pathetic stars. When I used a star cookie cutter, they were totally mashed. When I attempted to cut them free hand, their misshapen appearance made them look like they belonged at a party with Charlie Brown's Christmas tree. Of course, when I went to help with the party at school the next day, my ugly duckling stars were put next to plates of perfectly formed supermodel stars. I still have no idea how those other mothers did them. For a moment, I felt a pang of maternal inadequacy. Then I laughed to myself and thought, "These women have way too much time on their hands." It was time to rethink which activities were really necessary in my life. I needed to be much more deliberate about where I was putting my time and my energy. I decided to try to follow Ann Lamott's example: "I live by the truth that 'No' is a complete sentence" (Lamott 2005, p.174).

When we carry this perfect mother syndrome into raising our children with autism, we add even more pressure and intensity to being their moms. In addition to having more to do than we can manage, we now have to do everything perfectly. We set ourselves up to fail by expecting to do more than is humanly possible.

Ann

In my work with parents of children with autism, I am frequently reminded of how hard parents can be on themselves, especially those parents who have young children. I am continually struck by the wonderful job they are doing with their children, but at the same time I see them overextending themselves with insane schedules and impossible expectations of themselves. They have their child involved in every therapy possible, every rainbow soccer team, social skills group, or playgroup, while trying to follow strict diets and vitamin regimens. They attend every conference or workshop on autism, every support group, and every school event. Is it our feelings of inadequacy as parents that drive us to perform our roles at this level of intensity?

Having spent the last 20 years parenting a child with autism, I know that level of intensity is impossible to maintain. I want to tell these parents that none of us are superhuman. We all have good days and bad days. Part of being a good parent is realizing that we are human and that it's okay to figure it out as we go and to learn from our mistakes. We have to be able to appreciate the hard work that we do and not be critical of ourselves if we have limits to what we can physically and emotionally handle.

Being a good enough mother requires that we lower some of our standards. Unless we are fortunate enough to have a child with autism who likes to clean our house, it is usually impossible to reconcile Martha Stewart sensibilities with raising a child with autism.

Maureen

It was hard, but I finally resigned myself to the fact my house would never be in the condition it should be. Justin was just too good and too fast at dismantling and scattering everything I labored to pull back together. I decided to follow the advice I saw on a kitchen magnet: Is there anything that can't be solved by the phrase "The hell with it?" My friend Deb suggested I adopt her philosophy of housecleaning. She told me, "I decided the condition of my house would make my friends feel way better about their own."

When Justin was younger, he swept everything from every surface or bookshelf. He took all of the pictures off the wall. Our house was so devoid of decorating touches that a neighbor once asked us if we were packing to move. It bothered me that our house looked so sparse.

I wish I had known then that, like many behaviors of autism, his need to clear off every surface would not last forever. Eventually he either lost interest or learned to tolerate more objects in his environment. Our house started to look like we had finally moved in. His room was the only place he continued to remove pictures. But I found a friend who painted murals on his wall, helping make the room look more inviting.

Autism adds layers of complication to our lives. We take care of ourselves when we simplify life whenever and wherever we can.

Maureen

Because Justin required such close supervision, I came to the end of the day feeling totally unproductive. Rob and I had decided that taking care of the kids was my priority, but there were still many things that simply needed to get done for our lives to have some semblance of order. I could not figure out how to manage Justin's care and accomplish the rapidly escalating list of regular chores. After much trial and error, I learned some practical ways to simplify my life.

Each night I made a "To do" list. Then I went through the list to eliminate whatever non-essential things I could find. I consoled myself that one day I would find more time, but for now I needed to stick with the basics. I also looked for things I could transfer to somebody else's list. Though I hated to ask, my neighbors and friends were usually willing to help. When they went out to shop, they incorporated some of my errands with theirs. They also included Michael and Patrick with their kids for many of their after-school and weekend activities. After eliminating or delegating items from my list, I decided on the three most important priorities for the next day. I reminded myself that, for now, being productive meant accomplishing those priorities and not completing everything else on my list. I tried to get some things done before Justin got up in the morning or right after he went to school.

I also tried to simplify errands so that any errand that involved waiting or crowds could be done when Justin was not with me. Because he loved to ride in the car, I converted as many errands as possible to "drive thrus": the bank, the pharmacy, the dry cleaner, the gas station, and his all-time favorite, the car wash. I tried to simplify in other ways. Justin would strip off his clothes frequently during the day and night. I bought clothes that he couldn't get off by himself – overalls during the day and pajamas specially made to zip up the back at night.

For meals we kept many a fast-food restaurant in business. I always intended to cook a month's worth of dinners during one intense cooking day in the kitchen, but I never quite pulled it off. When I did cook, I tried to prepare for dinner at breakfast. The crock-pot became my gourmet kitchen utensil of choice. With other household chores, I tried to involve Justin when possible. Over the years his chores included loading and unloading the washer, dryer, and dishwasher, and helping with simple cooking tasks. Of course his favorite was the salad spinner.

Justin did us a favor by requiring us to simplify our holiday traditions. There simply was not enough time. But what family would not benefit from eliminating some of the holiday excess? Our change started the year I exhausted myself to make a traditional Thanksgiving meal that none of my children would eat. In exasperation, I announced that I would not repeat the same menu for Christmas dinner. I asked them, "What would you eat?" In unison, Michael and Patrick hollered "Tacos!" And the First Annual Morrell Family Taco Christmas Dinner was born. When friends got word of the event, they wanted to be included. They each brought one of the essential taco ingredients. On Christmas evening, we had a houseful of "severely normal" preschoolers, assorted children with autism, and adults wearing sombreros, all surrounded by South American travel posters. We set up tables in our unfurnished living room and enjoyed tacos and the piñata. To this day, tacos are the Morrell family Christmas dinner of choice. Years later we moved two hours away from our Greensboro friends. To help us get settled in our new home, they brought us a real Thanksgiving dinner which everyone ate. We still share this holiday tradition with these three other families. Over the years we have added a few single friends and additional children with autism. It has become a great "family" celebration.

Parenting a child with autism is a labor-intensive type of parenting. While it can be emotionally difficult to have to depend on others, sometimes we need to accept some help.

Ann

I do not accept help well. I am uncomfortable letting others see what feels like my failings or weaknesses. I don't like admitting I even need help, much less accepting that help when it is offered. I know it is healthy and normal to reach out to someone for help when things are difficult, but it totally goes against my nature to do so. As much as I hated it, when Eric was first diagnosed and Sarah was a baby, I realized I couldn't do it all. I had to accept the help that was being offered. Fortunately, my family and my husband's family were offering to help. I'm not sure I would have been able to initiate asking them. Over time I realized that needing their help didn't mean I had failed in any way. I was human and could only do so much.

Sometimes we have to "volunteer" people to help us.

Maureen

When my kids were in middle school, they made the mistake of bitterly complaining about the lunches I made them for school. Hearing one too many complaints, I announced that I was officially out of the lunch-making business. I also decided to roll (no pun intended) that lunch-making time into an additional hour of sleep in the morning until Justin got up. I told Michael and Patrick that they were on their own to get up and out to the school bus without me. They quickly (and somewhat surprisingly) rose to the challenge. They did just fine with making their lunches and getting to school. I was thrilled to get these morning rituals off my "To do" list. I wondered what else I was doing for Michael and Patrick that they were quite capable of doing for themselves. I decided to scrutinize my list for other things that I could give up or delegate.

❋ Lesson 3: Respite opportunities can offer relief

Respite provides parents temporary relief from the daily responsibilities of caring for our child with autism. While we know that we need a break from caregiving demands, we can be reluctant to use respite services. Our hesitation may come from the belief that we are the only ones willing and able to provide care for our child. We doubt that anyone else can provide the level of supervision and support that our child needs. Besides, how do we train someone else to appreciate our child's unique and quirky ways? Our children may have trouble accommodating new people coming into their lives. Using respite may add to their anxiety and upset the status quo. Sacrificing our privacy by inviting new people into our home can add to our stress. So can the realization that we leave our most vulnerable child in the care of a relative stranger. Finally, the arrangements for respite can rival the intricacies of planning the Olympics. By the time we recruit, train, schedule, and (take out a loan to) pay for respite services, we feel too exhausted and too overwhelmed to leave. No wonder we decide that respite may not be worth the effort.

Despite all our hesitations, there are compelling reasons to persevere in using respite care. Respite gives us some breathing room in a life where we are often physically and emotionally winded. By taking a break, we can return to our responsibilities with renewed energy and strength. Respite allows us to step back from our lives and gain some perspective. It gives us the chance to get out from under those trees that obscure our view of the forest. It also provides us the time to nurture our other important relationships, including the need to nurture ourselves. By giving us restorative time, respite helps us be more balanced people, partners, and parents.

Our children with autism can also benefit from respite. We forget that our children may need a break from us as well. Respite gives them the opportunity to develop new relationships. We enlarge the circle of people who know and care about our child. Respite providers can help our children with autism build new skills. Sometimes they can nudge our children towards independence in ways that we never would have considered. Respite providers also add an additional level of safety for our child. In the event of a family emergency, we have someone available who is prepared to take care of our child. We are not as vulnerable to the effects of unpredictable family crises.

Maureen

When Justin was very young, I was fortunate to have family and friends who helped me with respite. My first regular sitter was a college student who came from a large family. I believe she was more confident and competent in caring for Justin than I was as an insecure mother. Our occasional overnight and weekend care came from my sister who lived a few hours away. She would meet us at the door with a basket of food and respond to our shell-shocked appearance with a sympathetic smile.

Once we graduated to agency care providers, I found it more stressful to use respite. It was a big leap of faith letting strangers take care of Justin, even when they were trained. I knew if I wasn't confident in their ability, I would worry the entire time I was away. I was also concerned that if the care providers did not know what they were doing, Justin could be aggressive towards them. On top of all this emotion was all the advance preparation – the emergency numbers, the pages of instructions, the preparation of special meals, etc. The logistics often had me in meltdown mode before our departure. My family learned to anticipate my tearful announcement that I could not go after all. I usually recovered by the time we left and was always glad that I went.

I overcame these obstacles by starting with baby steps. Getting away made such a difference in my mental health that I persisted despite my initial discomfort. I started with new workers for short periods of time until I was confident about their abilities. Over time the process got easier. I graduated to a weekend away. The ultimate was sending Justin to summer camp. The first time Justin attended a week at the Autism Society of North Carolina camp, I cried and called every day. I was convinced that neither he nor the staff would be able to cope. When I heard what a great week he had at camp, I realized that his resilience at being away exceeded my own. I grew so comfortable with the camp that I often used sitters to take him and pick him up so we could spend a full week on vacation. Rob said that eventually we might reach the point of driving slowly through the camp and just gently pushing Justin and his bags out of the moving car.

Whether respite will be helpful to families depends heavily on the quality of the respite care provider.

Maureen

Recruiting providers for Justin became my peak skill. I was always on the lookout for the best classroom aides, teachers, special education students, or school volunteers who might want to do respite. As Justin got older, I used staff from adult group homes because they often had the most training and the least angst about managing Justin's behavior. Good care providers often knew other qualified people, so my workers enlisted their friends. When Justin got a Medicaid waiver for respite services, I still identified the persons I wanted and asked the provider agency to hire them. Another good source of care providers was other parents, though it's a huge act of friendship to share. My friend Thea said she knew we were good friends when I gave her some names from my list.

Maureen

One of the things I dreaded was having to provide the training for new care providers. So I made the process easier by developing an "Everything You Wanted to Know About Justin But Were Afraid to Ask" book with all the history, current IEP, emergency numbers, behavior plans, etc. Luckily it often worked out that people who were leaving trained their replacements before they left.

We have been incredibly fortunate to have many care providers who stayed with Justin for several years. I tried very hard to make the job as appealing as possible by being flexible and appreciative. When I could, I also supplemented their salary to make it more of a living wage. While I was lucky attracting good people to the door, Justin did his part by the remarkable way he has of getting people to care about him. His charm somehow makes people overlook how difficult he can be, and makes them keep coming back.

As I found good people, my comfort level with respite services grew. At first I felt guilty about leaving Justin at home. Then I figured if I was going to feel guilty all the time anyway, I might as well feel guilty at the beach. Over the years I lost all my guilt as I realized how much Justin preferred his routines over the times we traveled together. After all, how could Justin not like staying home with another person who was totally focused on making him happy?

Respite also provided some positives that I did not expect. I found that Justin had enough of the typical child in him to be more independent and well-mannered for someone else than he was for his mother. For example, Justin loves to smell bottles of perfume, so his respite worker Tony now takes him to the cosmetic counter at the mall. All I can see is the potential for glass bottles being swept off the counter and shattered glass all over the floor. Tony insists Justin not only behaves well, but is a favorite with the women who work at the counter. (I think the fact that Tony is a kind and extremely good-looking man doesn't hurt their acceptance of Justin, either.) Because his care providers were more adventurous than I, Justin's horizons were broadened through his inclusion in their family reunions, church services, or community concerts and festivals.

Our respite workers have also been a source of support for Michael and Patrick by expanding the circle of people who care about their brother. This was brought home to me years ago when I asked my children to tell me their favorite Christmas tradition. I expected Patrick (as a young, somewhat materialistic child) to blurt out the most obvious: "Presents!" Instead, he said his most important tradition was having Chuck, our long-time care provider, spend Christmas morning with our family. Having respite providers has helped our entire family – and has expanded our definition of family as well.

Ann

With the increasing incidence of autism, there are also more siblings of children with autism. My experience is that siblings are often very caring and understanding individuals who may have a personal interest in helping others on the spectrum. My daughter Sarah has done babysitting for several families with children with autism and has spent a summer working at a day camp for children with autism. Maureen's son Michael was a wonderful peer buddy for a teenage boy on the spectrum. I know of several siblings who enjoy volunteering and working in the autism community. They often make excellent respite care providers for families.

✳ Lesson 4: It's important to take a break now and then

While weekend getaways are terrific, we don't have to leave town to give ourselves time for renewal. We can each discover our own personal antidotes to stress. The goal is to use activities that renew our energy and restore our strength. We recognize activities that "re-create" us by their capacity to distract us from our daily struggles. These are the activities that make time stand still.

Usually we know what we want to do to give ourselves a break. We just can't figure out how to work it into our schedule. The first step is to remember that taking time for ourselves is not a luxury, it is a necessity. The next is to recognize that habits of self-care can be slowly worked into our life by gradually adding them into our schedule.

Maureen

My favorite activities to rejuvenate myself all share a common characteristic. When I do them, I am focusing all my attention on doing one thing at a time. Activities that interrupt the multitasking demands of my life are almost always relaxing. Having one thing to do at a time feels like a mini vacation. I especially love the physical work of a garden. When things are going well in my life, I get absorbed in the work and can appreciate the beauty in nature. When I am frustrated and upset with someone, I can use my pickaxe in the hard red clay soil of North Carolina and get out all my aggressions. I also enjoy reading books and listening to books on tape. It's refreshing to be absorbed in someone else's drama. I can live vicariously through the happy ending; if the conclusion is sad, I can count my blessings that at least there are *some* problems in life that I do not face. When the audio book narrator is especially good, I am soothed by being read to, connecting to the happy times of my childhood. I have been known to go for a ride in the car with Justin just so I can listen to the end of a book-on-tape.

Working in these activities that nourish our spirits is a funny thing. When we are not doing any of them, we are absolutely convinced we have no time to spare in our schedule. Yet when we do them, they magically expand the time in our day to the point where we wonder why we ever thought it would be so hard to accommodate them.

Ann

Maureen and I were recently speaking to a group of parents about our lives with autism. During the question and answer period someone asked us what we did for ourselves in addition to being parents of kids with autism. I told the audience member that I work (in the autism field), that I write (books and articles about autism), and that I volunteer (on the Board for the Autism Society of North Carolina). When I said all that, I realized she was still waiting for an answer about what I do that is not related to my son with autism. My professional career and my volunteering activities are things I do for myself, but they all started because of the autism in my life. Some may think that I spend too much time in activities related to autism, but I don't feel as though autism defines me. I also like to read, travel, cross-stitch, and go to movies. I know when I need a break from autism, and I make myself take those breaks.

✳ Lesson 5: It's a relief when our sense of humor returns

A parent's sense of humor can be a temporary casualty of the diagnosis of autism. Emily Ballance, a professional speaker and licensed professional counselor, spoke on stress and humor at the 2005 Autism Society of North Carolina Annual Conference. She reminded us that stress, worry, and anxiety associated with autism can cause a debilitating disease: Hypohumorosis, the silent killer of fun (Ballance 2005). At the time of the diagnosis, parents may believe that humor, like sleep, joy, and peace of mind, has left our lives forever. We don't realize that while we may initially have trouble rediscovering our sense of humor, it usually has a way of finding its way back to us.

Maureen

I can't really remember when I regained my sense of humor. I know when Justin was little I found nothing amusing about my life. I thought raising a child with autism was serious business and the only emotional release (besides yelling) that I used on a regular basis was crying. But somewhere along the line I got tired of crying. Perhaps my life was proof of the adage that tragedy plus time equals comedy. My life felt so absurdly chaotic and out of control that I just had to laugh.

Having friends in the same situation helped me discover the humorous sides of my life. Our conversations often started with "You will not *believe* what happened today…", and we would be off and running about some situation that struck us as terribly funny. Being able to share our gallows humor reassured me that it was safe to joke about the difficulties of my life. Humor reduced my pain about Justin to a more manageable level. Like crying, it provided a way to release lots of sadness and worry. But laughing was so much more fun! Rediscovering my sense of humor made me feel that life was finally returning to normal.

Humor can be found in places we did not expect. Sometimes our children help us find our sense of humor through their refreshing honesty. A good friend of ours gave us permission to share a funny story about her son. When Alex was around 18 months old he had not spoken at all, not baby babble or "Momma" or "Bye, bye" – nothing. Because of the numerous ear infections he had had, his parents were concerned that he might have a hearing loss. They didn't know at the time that he would eventually be diagnosed with autism. Not too long after having tubes put in his ears, his mom picked him up one day to carry him to his high-chair for lunch. She was enthusiastically saying, "Time for lunch, Alex!" Alex suddenly said very clearly, "I don't want another g—damn peanut butter and jelly sandwich." His mom was shocked, to say the least. She called her husband at work and said, "Alex is talking! And he's talking just like you!"

Ann

One of my favorite stories about Eric happened when I was helping him prepare for his transition to college. We were having a discussion about time management, something that is typically very difficult for freshmen entering college. It is not easy for any student to know when to work and when to play. To begin addressing this, part of my strategy was to have Eric write up a list of things he could do during his free time at college. I thought it would help him to think about what activities he could do for fun. He wasn't really sure what college life would be like and he needed something to look forward to. We sat down with a piece of paper and pen, ready to create this list of things to do during free time.

I started the discussion by making a couple of suggestions that I thought Eric would like. I suggested he could go to the campus library and read books about animals or whatever interested him. He liked that suggestion and wrote it on the list. I also suggested he could walk over to a local park near campus where he could spend time outdoors. He also liked that suggestion and added it to the list. Then Eric looked up from the list with a smile on his face. I was excited that Eric was going to participate and suggest something to add to the list. He looked at me and calmly said with a smile on his face, "And if I have a girlfriend, we can have sex during our free time!"

⁜ Lesson 6: Friends can be life savers

Friendships make a huge difference in a parent's ability to cope. Every parent needs someone to occasionally tell you that you are doing a good job, to listen to you when you need to talk, or just to help you feel less alone. In addition to encouragement, sometimes what we need from our friends is honesty, someone to tell us when we are being unreasonable or unrealistic. Occasionally friends can also distract us from our stressful lives and provide us with the opportunity just to be ourselves. Friendships can be affected once our child is diagnosed with autism. Our lives are so busy taking care of our child's needs and the needs of our family that there can be little time for anything else. It is easy for parents of children with autism to put friendships in the "would be nice if I had time" category.

Ann

I remember during the first year or so following Eric's diagnosis the only new people I ever seemed to meet were in the waiting rooms of speech and occupational therapy offices. We sat there with our children, who may or may not have been wreaking havoc at the time, waiting for our appointments and checking each other out. As we tried to diagnose each other's children, we would briefly make eye contact and smile. We all knew we weren't thrilled to be there and that we were worried about our kids. Sometimes conversations would start and we would make a connection. For ten minutes we would have great conversations about where to take our kids for hair cuts or to buy shoes or how long it had been since we'd had a good night's sleep. Then the receptionist would call one of our children's names and the connection would be broken until the next time we crossed paths at appointments. These friendships were ridiculously brief but meaningful just the same. I don't remember the names of the fellow moms I met in those waiting rooms, but I remember the connections we shared.

Friendships that exist before autism can change after the diagnosis. Sometimes it is just difficult for a parent of a child with autism to continue in a relationship with someone who does not have autism in his or her life. They may have a harder time finding common issues because their day-to-day lives have become so different. The friend without a child with autism may feel uncomfortable and not know what to do to help or what to say. Some parents of children with autism have difficulty being around their friends with typical children. It can remind them of how different their own lives are and what they might be missing.

Ann

My relationships with some of my friends changed following Eric's diagnosis. I don't think it was anyone's fault. It just happened. Some friendships gradually fizzled out because we didn't have lives that overlapped any more. My life had changed drastically as we added therapies, special schools, and support groups to our already busy days, and it was hard to make the time to contact my old friends. I also found it wasn't as comfortable for me to be with some of these friends after the diagnosis. I didn't want to, but I frequently found myself comparing Eric to my friends' children. When we were together he stood out. It was impossible not to notice the odd things he was doing and what he wasn't doing like the other children. When some of my friends tried to help me, it felt like they were feeling sorry for me. Their "How are you doing?" greeting always seemed tinged with sympathy. There were friends who tried to help by sending me articles about new therapies for autism, or they would make comments like, "I'm sure it's not autism and he will be fine." I didn't want to hear it wasn't autism and I didn't want to know about "cures." That didn't help me. The friends who stayed with me were the ones who didn't try to fix things and who didn't always feel sorry for me. They were the ones who said, "I know this is hard. I'm here if you need me." That's all.

Maureen

Justin's arrival in my life did not change my relationship with my childhood friends. Being confessors and advisors long before Maureen FitzGerald became Maureen Morrell, our histories wound together through all sorts of good times and bad. They have kept me grounded throughout most of my life. Despite the separations imposed by geography, they possessed a special power to slide between me and my grief.

With friends who came after Justin, the test of whether the friendship would last was largely a matter of energy. If the friendship needed lots of time and attention, it was likely the relationship needed more than I was able to give it. The friendships that continued were the flexible and low-maintenance ones. These friendships could accommodate my periods of self-absorption, unreturned phone calls, missed appointments, and the emotional roller-coaster ride that was my life. Luckily I kept many low-maintenance friendships and they enriched my life in indescribable ways.

For emotional support on issues with Justin, I usually relied on other "autism moms" whose experiences mirrored my own. But I also had friends who could empathize and support me without first-hand knowledge of my experience as Justin's mom. Invariably, they had experienced unexpected events in their own lives. Their familiarity with the struggles to rebuild after loss had imprinted them with the ability to recognize me as one of their own.

I also enjoyed my friends whose place in my life had absolutely nothing to do with autism. These were friendships developed in the world of our "severely normal" children and revolved around the shared world of school, sports, church, and the neighborhood. While their children knew Justin from coming to our house, these parents knew next to nothing about his life. It was a relief to have part of my life not focused on Justin's needs or on autism.

Parents of children with autism often find support and friendships with other parents in similar circumstances. There are support groups for autism and mentoring programs in many communities that can provide opportunities for us to connect. A parent of a newly diagnosed child can benefit from meeting another parent who can share advice and knowledge about resources in the community. A fellow parent of a child with autism may share similar experiences and feelings. Other parents often just seem to "get it." What a relief it is for us to visit a friend and not have to worry about what odd thing our child may do or what that person will think if our child has a meltdown. The friendships that can develop between parents of children on the autism spectrum can provide crucial support.

Ann

How do I describe my friendships with other moms of children with autism? These are the people who know the real me. These are the friends I call when Eric does something great or when Eric is struggling. We all understand that we aren't "Super Moms" simply because we have a child with a disability. We can be honest with each other about our self-doubts and the mistakes we make. These friends don't judge me or my choices. If I go to their homes with my family it's not stressful. I don't have to explain why Eric is only eating crackers and Cheerios and won't eat whatever the others are having. These are the friends who understand my life, and I understand theirs.

There is an initial bond that autism gave us, but our friendships are now based on much more than autism alone. The autism connection made it possible for us to meet, to support each other, and to develop personal relationships in addition to the autism issues we share. Now, we may rarely talk about the autism in our lives when we are together. But if things get difficult or if we are going through a personal crisis with our children, we know that we will be there for each other. That is what makes these friendships special to me.

Maureen

I share Ann's gratitude for what other mothers of children with autism have contributed to my life. The opportunity to "howl a bit" with people who know how I feel has been an irreplaceable consolation in my life (Hax 2005). Our friendships assure us that we are not parenting without a net.

Ann

I was at the beach with my family recently and a woman approached me while I was sitting in my chair reading. She very nicely said, "I hope you won't think I'm being too personal, but is that your son over there?" Eric was enjoying the beach; running back and forth at the water's edge, occasionally just standing there enjoying the feel of the water on his feet. I said, "Yes, that's my son." She said, "Does he have autism?" When I answered yes, she quickly said, "My son has autism, too," and pointed him out to me in the neighboring group of people on the beach. We struck up a conversation and immediately had a connection that had nothing to do with the functioning level of our children or their ages or what therapy we used. That day on the beach we were strangers who discovered we were members of the same club; not a popular club to join, but a club just the same. Though our children might be very different, we knew we had paid the same dues to join that club (Palmer 2006).

Our friends may not know what to do or say to us following our child's diagnosis. It is hard for them to know how to help and how much to help because everyone reacts differently and grieves in his or her own way. Sometimes the best thing friends can do is to stand by if needed, but not try to fix or direct anything. Probably the best way to know how to help a parent is by just asking what you can do.

Maureen

Sometimes our most helpful friends are known by what they don't do. My closest friends did not try to fix my life by advising me not to worry. They didn't gloss over my struggles by sharing stories of how other people had it much worse. They didn't feel they needed to defend God, trying to explain away the mysteries of why innocent people like Justin suffer. In fact, my friends often helped me the most by not talking about autism at all. It somehow showed me their faith in my ability to cope. They intuitively knew the truth of what an exasperated friend once told me: "I wish my friends would just shut up and bring me a casserole."

The eminently practical help of my friends was a powerful symbol of their presence and support. When I felt alone on the weekends that Rob was on call, I could have a quick cup of tea with Jim and Mary while Justin dismantled their playroom. I knew when I had to get Justin out for a walk at some obscenely early morning hour, Kathy would cheerfully join us. I had friends like Pat who absorbed Michael and Patrick into her family to diminish the chaos in my home. Or Sandy who folded them in with the care of her newborn twins and five other children, while I took Justin off for an evaluation. When Kathy heard the fatigue in my voice, I knew she would show up at my door with a meal. (What she *doesn't* know is that I sometimes sounded tired just to get her to cook one of her gourmet meals for our family!)

The friends I have relied on over the years have put these words into action:

> What you learn as you grow older and life sets you in ways for which you are never prepared, is that showing up matters. The simple, unremarkable, unheroic act of being there, bearing witness, saying in one way or another: I am with you. (Goodman and O'Brien 2000, p.232)

This is the best definition of friendship that we have found.

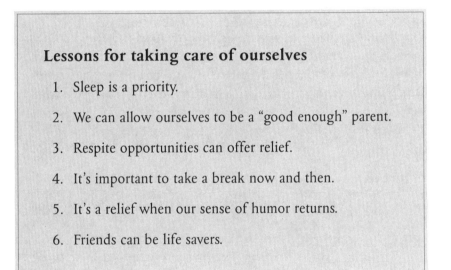

Lessons for taking care of ourselves

1. Sleep is a priority.

2. We can allow ourselves to be a "good enough" parent.

3. Respite opportunities can offer relief.

4. It's important to take a break now and then.

5. It's a relief when our sense of humor returns.

6. Friends can be life savers.

Chapter 7

Finding Our Way

When our children are first diagnosed, we are overwhelmed with what we don't know and need to know in order to help our child. We may go to the internet or to the library and anxiously search for the right information that applies to our own situation. With the increasing media attention to autism and the explosion of information on the internet, parents find themselves having to hack through a jungle of information. Some of it is legitimate and some is not. We have to be investigators, evaluating all the different therapies, research studies, and possible cures. It doesn't help that the professionals can't agree on which therapies work best. Deciphering all the information we find, and then applying it to our own situations with our own children, takes time. We are obviously on a very steep learning curve when our children are first diagnosed.

Ann

One of the things I found to be especially frustrating was the lack of communication among the different agencies or programs that were working with my child. Each program was giving us different advice and strategies to help Eric, with little consideration of what another program might be doing. As a parent new to this and not confident at all in my knowledge of autism and the decisions I was making for my child, it only deepened my feelings of inadequacy.

One day I was observing my son's speech therapy session through a two-way mirror with the director of the program. He told me that the key to improving my son's language would be to change all his routines, thereby making Eric ask for what was missing or verbalize his feelings about the changes. What the director was not considering was that my son was also being served by a program that emphasized using structure and routines to help Eric understand what was expected of him and to bring some predictability to his chaotic world. The structure we had been using at home had been helping with Eric's behaviors and frequent meltdowns.

I respected both programs and was appreciative of their efforts to help my child. But on that day, I followed my instincts that my child would fall apart if I changed all his routines. I knew that the routines he had were comforting to him, and changing them all at once would only create more behavior issues to deal with. I went with my instincts and my knowledge of Eric and stuck with the strategies that had been working for our child and our family.

Maureen

When Justin was first diagnosed I found that the advice meant to encourage me actually had the opposite effect. Professionals and older parents reminded me that I was the expert on my child. I knew this was meant to make me feel included as a valuable member of the treatment team. But the thought that I was the expert on Justin only added to my already sizable panic. If I was the expert, then we were in much deeper trouble than I had originally believed. I was also advised to trust my instincts. I knew that was sound advice, but I could no longer remember just what trusting my instincts meant. My survival instincts were already in overdrive. The momma bear in me often provided me just two choices of action: either get out of Dodge or rip somebody's head off. Neither option was very helpful in getting Justin the help that he needed. Then there was the suggestion to "trust your gut." I understand that the wisdom we find in our body is often ahead of our intellect. But when I was not in panic mode, I went through the motions of my day feeling shut down and numb. Finally there was the suggestion to "listen to your inner voice." I knew that I had one, but living with someone with autism made it hard for me to hear it. The only voices I heard were from the outside giving me confusing and conflicting advice. If I managed to find the time and the quiet to sit and listen to my inner voice, all I heard was a ticking clock warning me that Justin was falling irreparably behind and that decisions about treatment should have all been made yesterday.

Eventually I found the wisdom and truth in all this advice. Trusting my instincts, checking my gut reactions, and listening to my inner voice have been important guides in finding my way. What was missing in the advice that I received was a time frame. Grieving made accessing my inner resources difficult. With time and repeated deep breaths, I grew more confident in using my internal resources to evaluate the external information. With experience I decided which treatment I would use and which I would leave unexplored. As I came to understand Justin's brand of autism better, I eventually did grow to be the expert on my child. Living with him 24/7 gave me all the coursework for my Ph.D. in Justin Morrell.

We found our way by reconciling the outside information we gathered with the inside wisdom of our hearts, heads, and guts. This was (and is) an evolving process. Eventually we gained speed, skill, and a measure of confidence in deciding which treatment and educational approaches were right for each of our children.

Early on we thought that choosing strategies for treatment or education was a "black and white," "either/or" process. Either you picked a behavioral approach or a developmental approach. Either your child learned all he had to learn by the age of five or his life after five would go nowhere. Adolescence was either all good or all bad. Either you worked on academic skills or you worked on functional skills. The list went on and on. As our autism learning curve started to level off and we were able to trust our instincts, we discovered our black-and-white beliefs about autism were limiting our ability to explore all our options.

This chapter discusses where we think the prevailing wisdom is too black and white. We do not see the prevailing wisdom as completely wrong, but it frequently fails to tell the whole story. When important aspects of the whole story are omitted, many young parents today are more panicked and guilty than they need to be. These are the lessons we wish we had known when we were new mothers. These are the lessons that have surprised us the most. In discussing what we have learned, we will undoubtedly challenge someone else's closely held beliefs. So we will reiterate that the only expertise in the world of autism that we claim for ourselves is the expertise gained from our own experiences.

✳ Lesson 1: Early intervention is not the only key to the future

A promising hope for reducing the challenges of autism is "a growing body of evidence that early and appropriate intervention may indeed have a positive impact on overall outcome" (American Academy of Pediatrics, Committee on Children with Disabilities 2001, pp.22–3). Professional and parental experience (and basic common sense) would agree. Early intervention offers strategies for decreasing interfering behaviors and teaching specific skills. By including parents as part of the treatment team, early intervention helps build our abilities and confidence in helping our children succeed. Early intervention helps the entire family by connecting us with resources that help support the quality of family life. It is not surprising that early intervention is the first step parents take to help their child. And it is not surprising that the media focus so much attention on early intervention as the key to success for our children with autism.

We believe that what is missing in the discussions about early intervention is the recognition that the years before the age of five are not the *only* years when interventions can make a difference. Learning does not stop at age five. In fact, our children are continually learning, whether they are 2 or 22. We have found there is no time limit on building our children's skills for the future.

Ann

When Eric was diagnosed just before his third birthday, the currently required early intervention programs were not offered by the schools. Whatever we wanted for Eric we had to find, arrange, and pay for ourselves. There were no early intervention case managers to help us negotiate the choices that were available. We chose the therapies and programs we thought would best meet Eric's needs and fit our family's lifestyle.

Eric received private occupational and speech therapy each week. He attended two preschools, one for "typical" kids and one for children with speech and language difficulties. We made weekly visits to our local TEACCH center where Eric received help with communication, social skills, and behavioral strategies. I also worked with him one-to-one at home whenever I could fit it into our busy schedule. Like many parents, I felt the need to pursue every intervention that was possible and appropriate for Eric.

All the early interventions we received were chosen with the following criteria in mind: the cost, the distance from our home, whether it could be worked into our family schedule, and whether Eric could tolerate it. We relied on other parents of children with special needs and the professionals who were helping Eric to advise us about which strategies might help. When we considered new therapies we often had to rely on our instincts about whether the intervention was legitimate and would help Eric.

I have no doubt that these early interventions helped Eric. But the strategies and interventions that continued in his elementary and middle school years benefited him as well. The skills he learned in the self-contained autism classroom when he was six and seven years old enabled him to be included in regular education settings in later years. In middle school Eric learned crucial organizational skills that made college a possibility for him. Now, as a young man, he has become more flexible and more social than I ever would have imagined. Early intervention was important, but at the age of 22 he continues to surprise us as he learns new skills that we never thought would be possible.

Maureen

When Justin was diagnosed I held some of the blackest-and-whitest beliefs about early intervention possible. I was the director of nursing for an interdisciplinary project for high-risk and premature babies born at a general hospital. My position, and all my educational and professional work to that point, supported my belief that intervening early was the key to success for children at risk. So when Justin was diagnosed, I approached all the treatment and educational services with the absolute conviction that everything Justin needed to learn had to be learned by age five.

By the time Justin turned five, I was filled with despair. His progress had been excruciatingly slow and there were huge gaps in the skills that he needed to manage his life. He was nonverbal and unable to communicate what he needed or wanted. His behavior was maddeningly perseverative, unpredictable, and often self-injurious and aggressive. He was uninterested in and unable to use the toilet. He could be affectionate and loving with me, his dad, and a limited number of other adults, but, beyond that, other people and the usual interests of children his age held little appeal. I continued to pursue all the best available treatment and education services, but in my heart I stopped expecting that he would ever learn anything new.

Yet the truth is that all of Justin's important skills were learned after age five. Justin's greatest communication breakthrough was to come at age eight, when he finally stopped using tantrums to communicate and physically took us to what he wanted. At age ten, after years of two people supporting him on ice skates in what we called the two-person drag, Justin put on his skates and practically did an Olympic performance across the ice. By the time he was a pre-teen, he had riveting eye contact and clearly communicated his desire to connect with other people. Today he is often the unofficial nonverbal Wal-Mart greeter to visitors at the farm where he lives. While still occasionally problematic, his behavior is better and he is no longer the most high-maintenance person in the group. When former teachers or consultants see him today their first response is often, "Who would have thought Justin could do...?" It seemed as he got older he finally began to understand the world and to focus. It seems as though he is learning more now. His early years were not the only window of opportunity that existed for learning or intervention. Justin, like many other adults with autism, appears to be a lifelong learner.

The concept that individuals with autism can be lifelong learners is often eclipsed by the attention devoted to early intervention. However, it is a topic of great interest among parents of adolescents and adults with autism, and the professionals who work with them. Parents and professionals alike are often surprised and delighted by the progress in learning they observe in these individuals. In an informal poll we have asked many parents of an adolescent or adult with autism at what age their children learned the most. Invariably, they respond that, regardless of the approach, the adolescent and adult years have been the times of greatest learning. This mirrors our experience as well. We are not saying that later learning is better than early learning. No doubt the progress made by adolescents and adults grows from the foundation that is laid when they are young. But we are curious why so many of the children with autism whom we have known were "late bloomers." It raises questions in our minds about how the incremental and cumulative aspects of learning, developmental readiness, and maturation influence the learning process for individuals with autism. Perhaps as individuals with autism age and gain experience, they become less afraid, less overwhelmed, more confident, and more flexible. Perhaps this frees up some energy and focus for learning new skills that they were unable to access when they were young. The exploding research on the elasticity of the brain is promising for all individuals with autism, no matter what their ages. We are fortunate to have the realistic hope that lifelong learning will provide new opportunities for our children to improve their lives.

Ann

As the coordinator of a parent mentor program for parents of children with autism, I meet and work with parents of young, newly diagnosed children. I have seen the pressure these parents can put on themselves to try every therapy or every diet. They often feel the need to work with their child constantly to help him or her "catch up" or reach a particular milestone, often not taking the time to also enjoy their child. (I was guilty of this myself.)

Imagine the guilt parents feel when their children are diagnosed after the window of time that would include early intervention. They often blame themselves for not knowing something was wrong earlier or for losing valuable time in which to help their child. But my guess is that they weren't sitting on their hands before their child was diagnosed. Maybe they didn't have their child enrolled in early intervention programs or special therapies, but most likely they were stimulating them, nurturing them, and helping them in all the ways parents do naturally with their children.

✳ Lesson 2: There is no one right therapeutic approach for every child with autism

We understand and respect parents' needs to try any treatment or therapy that could possibly help their child. Because each child with autism is unique, the treatments and strategies families use must be individualized to find the most successful ones for that particular child. Parents know firsthand the truth of the adage, "When you have met one child with autism, you have met one child with autism." There is incredible variety in the nature and severity of any particular expression of autism spectrum disorder. So it makes sense that one educational approach or treatment will not work for all children. As Dr. Marie Bristol-Power writes:

> Since genetic, infectious, neurological, immunological, and possible environmental influences have been implicated in autism, no one is naïve enough to suggest that any one cause will account for all cases of autism, nor that any one treatment or "cure" will be sufficient to deal with all of its manifestations. Autism and the enormous variability among individuals with autism might be better understood as a class of disorders. Solving the puzzle of autism will be like peeling an onion, one layer at a time. (Bristol-Power 2000, p.16)

The various educational and treatment approaches all attempt to reduce the challenges of autism by decreasing interfering behaviors and developing specific skills. We have friends who have successfully relied on using one behavioral or developmental approach. However, what we have found with our own sons is that sometimes a combination of thera-peutic approaches can be helpful. There are many treatments and strate-gies that can be used together, or that can reinforce each other, to help an individual with autism. What is not always obvious at the outset is that approaches are not necessarily mutually exclusive. Rather than either/or, the most successful may be a combination of different approaches.

Maureen

Like many new moms, I faced the reality of not having enough hours in the day to accommodate our lives after autism. With Rob in the throes of medical school, I was the engine pulling our family train as our family breadwinner, chief cook and bottle washer, and Justin's primary care-giver. Life revolved around Justin's numerous therapy sessions and all the recommended follow-up work to be done in the evening at home. My engine was rapidly losing steam as I reached the end of my day. I would be left feeling overwhelmed, frustrated, and exhausted. I felt I was doing a terrible job managing all of the responsibilities in my life. I didn't see how we could keep living as we were.

A friend, who was also a special education teacher, offered a sugges-tion that led to one of the most important epiphanies in my life. She said, "You spend an enormous amount of your time, energy, and money on treatment and education for Justin. Maybe as his mom you should try to enjoy him more and work with him less." I realized that up to that point I was relating to Justin more as his nurse than his mom. I was treating him like a patient who needed fixing instead of like a child, who despite his profound disabilities was still just a child. I decided to look at our life through this different lens my friend had suggested.

The first thing I did was to stop all the homework that was forcing Justin and me into a contest of who would be the first and the loudest to leave the table kicking and screaming. I decided to really observe him over the next several weeks and to attempt to look at life from his point of view. I learned many things I had missed when I was working with him all the time. For example, working on tasks informally on the floor or the bed was more effective than the structured work at the table. It was clear he also needed more time than he was usually given to respond to requests or directions. He was more likely to follow directions given in a humorous tone of voice. When I used a monotone or an authoritative tone of voice, he was more likely to get self-injurious or aggressive. I learned that he is both a visual and a kinesthetic learner. Visual cues and getting up and moving around frequently between tasks helped keep him calm.

I asked the professionals to help me translate their recommendations into practical ways I could perform them at home. So Justin and I started practicing things like turn-taking and learning to wait while cuddled up sharing my cup of hot tea. We also practiced using silly games, physical play, or the activities of daily living like cooking and laundry as the vehicles for teaching new skills.

As a result of some of these changes, Justin seemed to learn more quickly with less drama and fewer disruptive behaviors. Reducing the intensity and formality in teaching him skills helped me work with Justin with more enjoyment than dread. I also realized that to provide Justin the long-term support he would need, I needed to take better care of myself. Slowly I forced myself to add more time for self-care.

Over the years I have used different combinations of developmental, behavioral, and biological approaches with Justin. All of them have had their benefits. All of them had their limitations. TEACCH methods were great in providing structure and visual cues for learning practical skills. Justin's disruptive behavior required the incorporation of specific behavior management techniques. While I never heard about "Floortime" when Justin was young, I used many of its principles in building on Justin's desire to connect and relate socially. Over the years I tried alternative therapies if they met my criterion of "Can't hurt, might help." I saw no appreciable difference in vitamin therapy or the gluten-free, casein-free diet. Medications for seizure control, behavior management, and recurrent gastrointestinal distress, however, proved to be helpful adjuncts to all the treatment and educational approaches we used.

My method in deciding which treatments to employ is not meant to be a model for anyone else. Comparing choices in treatment approaches from the past to those available today can be like comparing apples to oranges. In addition, there seems to be considerable variations under the broad categories of behavioral and developmental therapies related to how the programs are implemented. Parents all make decisions about what treatments to use based on very personal assessments of benefits and costs to their child and their family.

I am aware that lowering the intensity of our treatment approaches may have cost Justin the chance to learn specific skills. But I am also convinced that the cost was counterbalanced by the benefit of not having autism treatments consume every available minute. Over the long term I was willing to sacrifice some intensity in the autism treatment approach for the greater benefit I saw in keeping Justin surrounded by a strong, committed, still-married set of parents and healthy, caring, non-resentful siblings. Whether or not this was the best way is almost beside the point. It was the only way I could find to help Justin and keep our family together.

We can't help but feel that our child's outcome will be drastically affected if we don't receive the "right" services during the early years. But what are the right services? We can't possibly know which intervention is going to be the key for our particular child. Does that mean that we have to try them all?

The following are some things to consider when deciding which treatment and educational approaches to follow.

(a) First, do no harm

Performing even a cursory historical review of what passed for therapeutic treatments for autism provides the rationale for the rule: "First, do no harm." The common sense wisdom that "If it sounds too good to be true, it probably is" needs to apply, even when we are desperate for a miracle cure. Parents have the right and the obligation to question the evidence behind any recommended treatment or educational approach.

(b) Watch out for red flags

Be wary of evangelical proponents of any autism treatment. Signing up for a therapeutic treatment program should not make you feel like you're joining an exclusive religion. If you feel bullied or pressured into adopting an educational or treatment approach, walk away. If you are told the treatment's failure to deliver the expected results was your fault, run.

(c) Gather information with an open but questioning mind

There is a staggering amount of information about autism currently available. Our recent web search (for the word "autism") on Google revealed 6,310,000 autism-related references. While this information can serve as a valuable resource, it can also confuse more than it clarifies. Common sense dictates that we shouldn't believe everything we google. Anecdotal information on the internet, while deeply affecting and often compelling, still comes from individuals we have not met in person. The information from personal testimonials may not generalize to our specific children. Anecdotal information does not provide a big enough basket to put all of our eggs in. It should not be the sole basis for choosing a therapeutic or educational approach for our children.

(d) Connect in person

We find there is no substitute for gathering information about autism by connecting to others in person. Consult with different professionals and other parents. Reserve some time in your day to really reflect on their information and advice. Determine if the outside information you receive resonates with your intuition and your knowledge of your child. Develop a circle of professional and parent advisors and use them as a sounding board throughout your child's life.

(e) Make mid-course corrections when needed

Once parents commit to a particular treatment or educational approach, they should try to aim for a balance between two opposing temptations. At one extreme, we limit our options by becoming evangelical that this treatment is the only approach to pursue for our child (and for every other child with autism as well). At the other extreme, we drive ourselves crazy by worrying about all the treatments we did not pursue. It is both maddening and encouraging that we can modify, change, and blend treatment approaches. However, all new treatments should follow the safety rule of can't hurt, might help.

(f) Trust your own instincts

It helps to remember that the treatment approaches we follow may have as many unique variations as do our children. We should try not to feel inadequate or threatened by the choices of other parents. Movie director Billy Wilder once advised, "Trust your own instinct. Your mistakes might as well be your own, instead of someone else's."

(g) Share different points of view

The parents and professionals who have successfully advocated for increased attention and funding for research have our admiration and appreciation. It appears a clearer picture of autism is emerging as investigators connect the dots of experiential and research information. From our point of view, differences in the understanding and treatment of autism can actually move us forward in our search to find the most effective ways to help individuals with autism and their families. However, it is common for both parent and professional believers of particular approaches to get locked into controversy and hostility with believers of different approaches. As Dr. Marie Bristol-Power has said:

> It would be an impoverished research field indeed if everyone agreed… In the face of [such] controversy, we must continue to be willing to stimulate divergent research and to hold all players accountable to the rules of evidence. The complexity of the puzzle of autism requires collaboration across disciplines and groups. The best research will be conducted by individuals and agencies willing to tackle new challenges and data-test theories. They will also have to be humble enough to acknowledge the limitations of our knowledge and our methodologies. (Bristol-Power 2000, p.17)

(h) Consider both the professional and the approach

No matter what treatment or educational approach we select, its effectiveness depends on the skill of the professional who uses it with our child. The professionals who took the time to first get to know and understand our children were the ones who helped them the most. Based on their assessment and knowledge of our child, they blended the best elements from a variety of educational approaches to use with our child. This may be heresy to believers of black-and-white, either/or autism treatment and educational approaches. But, in our experience, the skill of the professionals working with our children was more important to our child's success than the educational or treatment methodology that they used.

Ann

In my work with parents of children with autism I frequently hear parents' anecdotal reports on the success of different therapies or treatments. Years ago it seemed that more parents were choosing one particular therapeutic approach and focusing 100 percent on that. Now I am seeing more and more parents who are finding that using a combination of different therapies, or pieces of different approaches, can be helpful. I know a number of families that use TEACCH methods primarily in the classroom, while at home the child receives Applied Behavioral Analysis (ABA). Sensory Integration Therapy and the gluten-free, casein-free diet, as well as other approaches, can be used successfully in combination with other treatments. The unique needs of each child often require parents to be creative and flexible in developing a program that best meets the individual needs of the child. Many are finding a combination of different approaches fits their family's schedule and lifestyle best.

✳ Lesson 3: Adolescence is not all bad

Consider this list compiled by parents of teenagers:

- Eats as if his stomach were a bottomless pit, raids the refrigerator at every chance, consumes quantities of junk food

- Needs to be reminded to bathe, wash hair, put on clean clothes, and comb hair and even when he does, he manages to look untidy

- Needs reminders to clean his room

- Has trouble managing money

- Parents never know what he is thinking or what is troubling him

- Spends much time each day lying in front of the TV. It takes a lot of encouragement and nagging to get him outdoors or involved in other activities

- Unsure of self

- Appears clumsy and awkward, drops things. Bumps into furniture. Walks in an ungainly manner. (Page 1980, p.2)

Does this list describe teenagers with autism or teenagers without autism? The answer is both. Teenagers with autism are in many ways like their peers who do not have autism. Some of the challenges parents of teenagers with autism face come with the turf of typical adolescence.

Parents of children with autism may find themselves worrying about the onset of adolescence long before it actually happens. We know adolescence can be a difficult time for all children and their families. So we assume it is going to be more difficult for a child with autism. We read about the onset of seizure disorders that can occur in adolescence, or the development of difficult, sometimes aggressive behaviors during those years. What we don't realize is by the time we are parents of adolescents, we are parents with an expanded set of skills.

Maureen

First I can confirm the expectation that, for some children with autism, adolescence can be tough. Justin's was. He started puberty early, around age 11. Soon after, he developed a seizure disorder. His behavior problems, which had been on the decline, reappeared with added intensity and persistence. It was a very difficult time for us all.

But, curiously, it was never as bad as I had imagined it would be given the autism worldview I had as a younger mom. Even when we considered temporary out-of-home placement for behavior management support, I felt that we would eventually get on the other side of our problems. This was because I was a different mother by the time Justin became an adolescent. By that time, I felt like an expert on my child. I was a more confident, informed parent with an extensive network of professionals and other parents who could advise me. Yes, I was back on the emotional roller-coaster, and there were times I would feel overwhelmed. But I'd ridden this roller-coaster before, and I knew it would not last forever. That made a huge difference in my ability to ride out the ups and downs of the adolescent years.

One of the alarming things about his adolescence was that Justin started giving up many of the favorite activities that we had always relied on in the past. I was thrown by his refusal to get into and out of the car or to spend any time outdoors. One day, after I wrestled him outside, he had a major meltdown. After wrestling him back to his room, I went outside to see if I could figure out what in the world had upset him so much. Just as I did when he was younger, I tried to get into his head and see the world as he did. After a few minutes I concluded that what upset him was probably related to what he heard. When I concentrated and tried to let go of my sensory filters, I heard the many noises of spring that I think he found painful – birds chirping, wind blowing, lawnmowers whirling, cars honking, and a muffler-less motorcycle roaring down the road. I recognized that the look on his face had been sheer terror. His sensory overload was combining with the increasing hormones of adolescence and resulting in high levels of anxiety. Who does not remember how excruciating the anxiety of adolescence can feel?

We were lucky that anti-anxiety medication helped Justin regain a large measure of control over his behavior during adolescence and beyond. He resumed most of his favorite activities. He surprised us by going through a period of learning new skills during this time. Our strategy of keeping Justin outdoors and physically active helped us get through this time, as did the comforting knowledge that parents of all adolescents (with or without disabilities) share – adolescence does not last forever.

In addition, we know that change is hard for our children with autism. How do we prepare them for the physical changes that are coming with adolescence?

Ann

I wanted to warn Eric in some way about the physical changes his body would be going through in adolescence. I spoke to him about how he would be getting taller and his voice would be getting deeper like Daddy's. I tried to use his father as a visual example of the changes to come and to emphasize that the process is normal and not a big deal. I didn't realize until much later that when I told Eric that he would be gradually changing into a man like Daddy, he literally thought I meant he was going to turn into Daddy. He thought he would one day physically change into his father and would no longer be Eric. Understandably he was scared and was waiting for the dreaded day of change. When I realized what he was thinking, I felt badly and quickly explained that he would always be Eric, but that his outside part was just going to very gradually change into a taller, hairier Eric. He could understand and accept this and no longer worried about the physical changes of adolescence.

Parents rarely get the opportunity to hear about the positive growth our children can go through during adolescence. Many of our sons and daughters with autism experience a period of increasing maturity during this time. They may become more flexible and have better self-control as they mature. They may show more social interests during the teenage years, which can lead to the development of better social skills. For the first time, they may show more independence and not rely as heavily on prompting from parents. Sometimes stomping to bedrooms and slamming doors can be a welcome sign for the parents of children who haven't stood up for themselves in the past.

Teenage boys and girls with autism are also protected in some ways from the dangers and stresses of the typical adolescent years. A socially withdrawn teen who is not a part of a close social circle may not be as susceptible to peer pressure. Also, if the teen is somewhat rule-bound, chances are he or she won't be sneaking out of the house at night or participating in underage drinking. Many of our adolescents on the autism spectrum who have sensory issues related to smell or taste are probably not going to begin smoking or taking drugs. Of course this doesn't mean that adolescents with autism don't have struggles with other challenges, because they frequently do. But during this time of change and uncertainty, it helps for parents to find those aspects of adolescence that may be positive for their children.

✵ Lesson 4: Functioning level is not the only predictor of success

Understandably, many parents are concerned about the functioning abilities of their children with autism and how much they will be able to achieve in the future. Even when our children are very young, we try to predict whether they will be able to communicate effectively, be independent, work, and develop relationships. These concerns help motivate us to access all the supports and help possible for our children. Many parents believe that the higher the cognitive abilities of the child, the easier their child's life will be and the more successful he or she will be in the future.

Our experiences with our own children and the experiences of many of our friends have shown us that there are challenges for *all* children with autism and their families, no matter where the child is on the spectrum. Having a child with Asperger Syndrome or high-functioning autism does not necessarily mean he or she will have an easier life or be more successful. We know adults on the spectrum with normal or above-normal intelligence who struggle with finding and keeping employment, living independently, and relating to others socially. We also know adults with autism who have mental retardation and low verbal skills but are able to work, live in a group setting with support, and have a full and active life that many would classify as successful.

Definitions of success are going to vary and what constitutes success for one child will be different for another. We need to focus more on the progression of our child over time and not on a final outcome. Our definitions of success for each of our children are going to change and depend upon how far they have come and how far they may still have to go.

Ann

One thing I have discovered since Eric has become an adult is that whether a child was previously labeled high- or low-functioning is less of an issue in advocacy efforts for our adult children. In public school there were more divisions among children on the autism spectrum based on their levels of disability. There were parents or parent groups who advocated for more services for those students who were in mainstreamed settings. There were other parents and parent groups who advocated for the needs of those students in special education settings.

My guess is that many parents feel they have to focus their energy on goals that, if achieved, will have a direct impact on their own child's situation. They may have little time or energy to advocate for services for the more general needs of all students on the autism spectrum. Whatever the reasoning, it is a shame that parents often find themselves divided in their advocacy efforts when a unified approach can frequently lead to better results.

Everything is very different once a child on the autism spectrum becomes an adult. Almost all of our children will need some level of support when they are adults due to the need for functional, social, advocacy, and independence skills in the adult world. There are also fewer resources and services available to *all* adults with disabilities, no matter what their functioning levels. Because of limited options and competition for services, the individuals on the higher end of the autism spectrum must often fight harder to defend their need for assistance. My experience so far is that parents of adults with autism, no matter where their adult children fall on the spectrum, soon realize the need to stick together and advocate for all of our adult sons and daughters. Functioning level does not seem to divide us as easily as it did during the school years.

✳ Lesson 5: Academic success is not everything

Many of our children with autism are visual learners and may do well academically. That is a wonderful strength and one that can open doors to opportunities for inclusion. However, academic success doesn't always mean the child is learning life skills. Being able to achieve academically, attend college, and get a degree does not guarantee successful employment or the ability to live independently. The time spent on pursuing academics needs to be balanced by time spent on learning functional life skills.

Ann

I was always thrilled when Eric met his academic challenges in school. When he was very young and reading at the age of three, I was consoled by the fact that he was reading ahead of the other kids his age. I needed to see some advanced abilities to compensate for all the areas where I knew he was lagging behind. However, when Eric was in middle school I realized that he could do algebra, but he couldn't go into McDonald's, buy his lunch, and know if he got the correct change back. It was then I realized that academic success was important in terms of having him included in regular education, but it wasn't necessarily going to help him as much as the life skills he required to be independent.

Nothing convinced me more of the importance of this issue than when we were preparing Eric for the transition to college. When we started to think seriously about all the things he would need to do independently and all the areas of day-to-day living that he had never experienced, we began to realize how much he needed to learn. If I had to do it over again, I would have begun earlier to focus on the functional skills that Eric needed to learn. I would have started earlier to teach him about self-help, money management, and household maintenance. The inclusion setting in school typically does not teach these kinds of skills in the regular curriculum, so it is up to parents to address these issues at home and in the community. As a parent it is easy to forget these more critical life skills when we focus too heavily on the child's academic strengths.

✳ Lesson 6: Not everyone wants to be cured

There is an increasing number of individuals on the autism spectrum who are advocating for their rights to be who they are, and not who others expect them to be. Many feel there are benefits to being on the autism spectrum and they should be welcomed into the neurotypical world for the unique and creative views they can contribute. They eloquently make the point that they do not think of Asperger Syndrome or autism as a disease, therefore they don't need a cure. They believe that individuals with autism, "with their obsessive attention to detail and eccentric perspective, can provide valuable insight and innovation" (Harmon 2004, p.A1). Rather than trying to suppress certain autistic traits, they feel people in the neurotypical world should simply be more tolerant.

Parents of children on the spectrum may have difficulty accepting this self-advocacy movement, especially if they struggle daily to help a child with severe issues that impact the child and the family. Our nature as parents directs us to do everything we can to rid our children of this condition that makes their lives so difficult. For our children who are not able to speak or communicate their views about this issue, we can't know how they feel about having autism or if they support our efforts to diminish the autistic behaviors that affect their lives. We can only try to respect the right of individuals with autism to be who they are and remind ourselves frequently to consider their perspective as we make choices to help them. We are fortunate to have the writings of self-advocates like Temple Grandin, Jerry Newport, Stephen Shore, Liane Holliday Willey, and others to help parents understand the point of view of individuals with autism.

Our friend Dave Spicer understands both sides of the debate between parents and self-advocates. He received his diagnosis of high-functioning autism (HFA)/Asperger Syndrome at age 46, following his son's diagnosis at age 8. Dave writes, "There seems to be a growing conflict between many parents and some autistic folks...try mentioning the word 'cure' and see what happens. It can be very polarizing." Concerned about the energy being consumed in this conflict, Dave offers a different way of viewing these issues. What if autism were considered "a neurological arrangement [with] all kinds of possibilities in it?" Of course, autism is often accompanied by difficult behavior issues, which Dave suggests we might consider to be "side effects." He is not minimizing the problems such behaviors can produce. He simply hopes that by reframing the discussion in this way, we might all be able to share a more balanced perspective on this perplexing condition, one which would allow for more civil dialogue and fewer lines drawn in the sand (Spicer 2005, pp.11–12).

Lessons for finding our way

1. Early intervention is not the only key to the future.

2. There is no one right therapeutic approach for every child with autism:

    (a) First, do no harm

    (b) Watch out for red flags

    (c) Gather information with an open but questioning mind

    (d) Connect in person

    (e) Make mid-course corrections when needed

    (f) Trust your own instincts

    (g) Share different points of view

    (h) Consider both the professional and the approach.

3. Adolescence is not all bad.

4. Functioning level is not the only predictor of success.

5. Academic success is not everything.

6. Not everyone wants to be cured.

Chapter 8

Dealing with the Public

In our society what others think of us or how well we conform to accepted norms can be very important. We want people to like us. We want people to accept us. As parents we especially want this for our children. When our child has a disability, acceptance by the public becomes even more crucial. How the public treats our children can directly influence their self-esteem and our own feelings about our abilities to parent.

For our purposes the "public" includes all those people we come into contact with who are not family and are not the professionals who care for our children. This would include our children's classmates, the police, the neighbors, the people in line with us at the grocery store, or the other shoppers in the mall. It includes all the strangers or slight acquaintances who don't know us, don't know our children, and probably don't know much about autism.

Why do we react to the responses of people who don't know us? How sensitive we are to the comments or judgments of others will depend on our personalities and our confidence in ourselves. In Chapter 3, we mentioned that siblings have personality styles that influence how seriously they regard other people's opinions about their sibling with autism. Parents probably fall into one of these three categories as well, varying significantly in the levels of hurt and embarrassment they feel when their children with autism are exposed to public comment. Those with Teflon personalities may be unfazed by other people's opinions, which tend to roll off their backs. For those with Velcro personalities, the feelings from public notice of their children may stick for a while, but eventually can be removed. But parents with Superglue personalities experience the public's real or perceived unkindness toward their children like a permanent bond.

Maureen

Michael and Patrick developed Teflon personalities regarding others' reactions to Justin's behavior. If this personality trait is genetic, then they clearly inherited this non-stick gene from Rob, who shares the same Teflon point of view. As a younger mom, I was firmly stuck in the Superglue category. My worries about public reactions to Justin's behavior felt like an enduring fixture in my life.

My own unique mixture of history and heredity left me with a tendency to exaggerate the importance of other people's opinions. I grew up looking outside of my family and myself for approval and validation. I worried about being liked and went to great lengths to make a good impression. When I was with Justin in public I felt like we made quite an impression – none of it particularly good.

I felt responsible for Justin's disruptive behaviors. I was like the elementary school child who feels guilty when the class misbehaves, even though she has done nothing wrong. My fierce momma bear attachment to Justin engendered a "you and me against the world" attitude, which helped me become his strongest advocate. But as a side effect, much of my life was being lived through Justin's. His successes and failures were somehow becoming my own.

Many parents share the tendency to overidentify with the public's reaction to their children. Attend any academic assembly or school sporting event and you can witness parents enjoying the opportunity to bask in their children's reflected glory. Over the years I have taken guilty pleasure in Michael's and Patrick's public accomplishments as if they were confirmation of my good parenting. But with Justin I realized that this process can work in reverse. Parents can absorb their children's failures as well. Justin's behavior made me embarrassed and ashamed.

I spent a lot of time agonizing over and apologizing for Justin's behavior during his early years. A simple remark from a kind teacher helped me stop. When I went to pick up Justin at preschool one day, his teacher mentioned he had bitten her earlier in the day. I began my usual intense litany of apologies when she stopped me. Looking me in the eye, she gently said, "It's okay, Maureen. You are not the one who bit me. You do not have to keep apologizing for Justin's behavior." It was one of those teachable moments when the right person says the right thing at just the right time to provide you an important insight.

Our culture tends to judge parents by the behavior of their children. Parents of any child, with or without a disability, may see the child's behavior in public as a reflection of their parenting skills. What parents are not proud of their child who sits quietly through a concert or behaves well when visiting someone else's home? When others compliment the good behavior of our children, aren't they really complimenting our successful parenting? Not only can parents be embarrassed by the behavior of their children in public, they may also feel a sense of failure at not being able to control the situation or prevent it from happening. Parents of a child with autism have to make frequent crucial decisions, deal with complicated behaviors and tiring therapies, and at the same time balance the needs of everyone in the family. It is understandable that we may feel inadequate as we tackle the constant stream of crises that can arise. When people in public react negatively to our children it can add to our pre-existing feelings of parental inadequacy.

Along with our personality traits, our sensitivity toward public notice of our children with autism can also be influenced by our personal histories. That sensitivity will depend in part on our own school experiences and our feelings about people who are different. And we can be more sensitive to the reactions of strangers because of our fears for our children – the fear that they will be rejected or, worse, taken advantage of.

For a parent of a child with autism, it is incredibly painful to hear someone in the grocery store make a comment about your child or see the judgmental looks of strangers when you're having a difficult time with your child in public. When you are already living with the many stresses of parenting a child with a disability, dealing with the public's response may be more than parents can handle sometimes. Parents of children with unpredictable behaviors may isolate themselves rather than take the risk of experiencing the negative reactions of people who don't understand.

The fact that autism is not immediately apparent can complicate things even more. As most children with autism have no obvious physical differences, people in the community may assume there is nothing different about them. Then, when the child exhibits an odd behavior or requires special assistance, other people may think that the child is intentionally acting out or that the parent is overreacting.

For those children on the autism spectrum who can be mainstreamed or included in programs for children without disabilities, there is often the concern that the child will stand out or need special assistance that will invariably attract the attention of others. At that point the question of disclosure about the disability can become an issue. Do you tell the professionals (teacher, administrator, coach, *et al.*) involved in the program? Do you want the other children to know anything about your child's differences? What about the parents of the other children in the program? Keep in mind that the child with autism may not want anyone to know about the diagnosis. If you don't disclose and the child has struggles, will there be someone available who understands why he or she is having difficulty and is able to step in and help?

Ann

I struggled with this issue throughout Eric's years growing up. His strengths enabled him to be included with "typical" peers at school and in programs outside of school. But he usually required some extra help, and his behaviors made him appear different from his peers. At school I felt comfortable disclosing Eric's needs, but for camps or short-term programs outside of school the decision was not so easy. If I told the people in charge about problems that could happen or assistance Eric might need, they might not accept him in the program. By not telling them about the autism, I was potentially keeping strategies from being used that could help prevent Eric from failing or having a problem. I wanted Eric to be as successful as possible and I didn't want to withhold the help that he might need to be successful.

Often there were uncomfortable moments with parents of other children in a class or at a camp who did not know about Eric's autism. They would ask me some generic question that, if I answered honestly, would reveal Eric's differences. (What grade is he in? Does Eric play any sports? Is Eric going with the other second graders on their field trip?) Sometimes Eric would "stim" or act odd in some way, and another parent would ask me what he was doing. I was always pretty open about Eric's autism when I needed to be, but I also avoided the conversation in situations that didn't require it. It was always a dilemma deciding who should know about the autism and who didn't have to.

We have had more than 20 years to respond to the reactions of strangers and to make the decisions about who to disclose to and what to say. Now that our sons are adults it is still difficult deciding how much information to share and it still feels bad when someone reacts unfairly to our sons. The many years of dealing with this have made us less sensitive to people's reactions which, in reality, usually don't matter. We have developed thicker skins toward the ignorant comments of others, and have even learned to use these experiences as an opportunity to educate them about autism. But it wasn't always this way, and, in the early years following the diagnosis, it was much harder to deal with the public's response to our children. The following are some of the strategies that have helped us.

❋ Lesson 1: It helps to find outings that work for the whole family

We always hope to have successful family outings with everyone having a great time and no problems. To help achieve this goal it is important to choose an activity that is a good "fit" for the child with autism and therefore less likely to be disrupted by problems. Because many of our children have short attention spans, we should take this into consideration when planning an outing. Choose places where waiting is short or not necessary at all. Find places to go that are related to your child's interests and skills so their attention will be more focused. It may also help the child participate if you choose activities that are fairly predictable and involve a routine each time.

Ann

Going to the movies was one of my favorite things to do with Eric and it was something all the children enjoyed. When Eric was little, he had some problems with the previews or "trailers" shown before the movie. The volume level was typically too loud and he would have to cover his ears. He also didn't like not knowing what previews would be shown and he would get anxious worrying about the possibility of seeing clips of scary movies. Sometimes we had to stand in the hallway outside the theater until the previews were over and then go to our seats. Eventually Eric was willing to sit through them, especially when he discovered that he actually liked some of the movies being previewed!

Eric loved all the animated Disney movies and would be completely enthralled from beginning to end. I know some friends who worry about their children not being able to stay in their seats through a movie. Eric wouldn't leave his seat during a movie if you paid him. We were in a movie one day and it was much scarier than we thought it would be. The movie was really too scary for my daughter and she wanted to leave. I leaned over and whispered to Eric, "This is too scary for Sarah. Do you mind if we leave?" Eric gave me a relieved but shocked look and said, "You mean we can leave?" He had been sitting there terrified and had never considered the possibility of being able to leave the theater.

It is equally important to realize which activities aren't good matches for your child with autism. Think about any sensory issues your child may have and choose places that would minimize those difficulties. Loud places with crowds of people may not be appropriate for some of our kids and should be avoided. Visually overstimulating places may be too much for some of our children. Think about safety issues as well. If your child is a "runner," will he or she be safe in this setting?

Ann

I have been surprised when I see classes of autistic students and clients from group homes on field trips to the state fair. Is there a more overly stimulating place possible for someone with autism? The loud vendors and music, the huge crowds of people, the strong smells of sausage, funnel cakes, and other assorted fattening fair food, and the blinking lights and colors are pretty overwhelming to me, and I don't have autism. How do they handle it? I often wonder if this kind of activity is the right choice for some of our loved ones with autism.

Sometimes an activity may not be appropriate for the child with autism but is something the rest of the family wants to do. Those are the times we have to think of other options so that the needs of others in the family can be met. One parent may need to stay home or do another activity with the child with autism, while the other parent does something different with the siblings. Sometimes a family needs to ask someone to stay with the child with autism while the rest of the family has an outing together. This is usually not our preference, but it can be necessary if that works best for the whole family. It is not fair to make the child with autism suffer through an activity he or she dislikes, nor is it fair to make a sibling do without just because the child with autism can't participate. Families need to consider what is best for *all* members of the family.

Ann

There were some outings that were never successful, especially when Eric was younger. Restaurants tended to be a bust unless it was a McDonald's with a playground. Eric didn't have the patience to stand in line or to wait for his food to be served. He wouldn't eat the food most restaurants offered and I would have to bring in food that Eric would eat. One day we were in a nice, non-fast-food type of restaurant for lunch. I had brought in a bag of McDonald's food for Eric to eat while the other children and I ate the restaurant food. While we were sitting there eating, the manager of the restaurant came up and informed me that they did not allow customers to bring in food from other establishments and asked me to please not do that again. There were three of us eating and paying for food from the restaurant. It seemed to me that we were helping their business, not hurting it. I decided not to visit that particular restaurant again. There were plenty of other restaurants that were more accepting and would allow us to bring in food for Eric.

✳ **Lesson 2: You need to prepare for all contingencies**

Preparation is an integral part of having a successful experience with our children with autism in public. When we prepare for all the possibilities that can occur, we increase our chances of having a pleasurable experience. It will involve some work on our part, but will make things easier in the long run. We need to think ahead about what our children will need while away from home, choose activities that we know have potential for success, and always have a backup plan.

We should take anything with us that may be needed on the outing. Think about what your child may request or need and what will be available where you're going. It never hurts to carry toys or objects with us that have some entertainment value for the child while waiting. These "comfort" items can also be used to calm our child if he or she starts to get upset. If we bring our own snacks and drinks, we can have them readily available. A change of clothes may also be important to have on hand.

What if things suddenly start going badly on the outing? Do we have a plan for getting out of the situation quickly and with as little trauma as possible? It helps to scope out the exits beforehand in case we have to make a quick getaway. Do we have enough adult help so that we can exit with our child with autism and not make everyone else leave?

Preparing for the worst scenario is never a bad idea. With luck, you won't need to implement a Plan B, but it's always wise to have one.

Preparing our children as much as possible is also important. You will need to prepare them in whatever way is most understandable to them, whether it is verbally or with a schedule, picture cards, objects, etc. Letting them know ahead of time where they are going can help them make the necessary transitions more successfully. Some children will benefit from a visual list or explanation of what they will be doing or if there are any rules they might need to follow. Transitioning away from a fun activity can also be a problem, so preparing our children for what comes next is important. Again, this needs to be communicated in whatever way makes sense to your child.

Maureen

Advance planning and flexibility were necessary for successfully including Justin in our family activities in the community. The first step was to try to evaluate his moods and plan accordingly. If he was having trouble managing his behaviors, we tried to pick activities that would not restrict his ability to move around. We also looked for activities that did not have large crowds or require waiting in line. For the siblings, we tried to make the activity sound desirable on its own merits and not present the activity as being the only one we could do because of Justin's behavior. So a hike in the state park was made more desirable by bringing a picnic lunch from the drive-thru lane of a fast-food restaurant. Or a swim at the lake was more fun when we found our own private beach near the outdoor picnic shelters that we rented or "borrowed" for the day. It was helpful having two adults and two cars just in case. When Justin was in a good mood we were often more adventurous. We might go to a museum, a shopping mall, or the bowling alley. While not an enthusiastic bowler, Justin was enamored of the bowling alley's ceiling fans. He also joined the rest of his family in the unshakable conviction that bowling alleys always serve the best french fries in town.

My Girl Scout sensibilities for being prepared (and the memory of a few disastrous outings when I was not) led me to certain routines for community outings. I tried to think through all the "what if " scenarios. I needed to know that I could leave with Justin quickly if necessary. So I drove and visited any new place we planned to go to with Justin. I checked out the closest parking, the entrances and exits, and the location of the bathrooms. Whenever possible I purchased tickets in advance to avoid waiting in line. I asked an employee when the building was least crowded. I also looked for the areas in the building to avoid; Justin did not need the temptations of an open food court or a gift shop filled with breakable items. I did not want to set Justin up to fail.

Another strategy I wish I had started earlier was frequenting the restaurants and shops that his school's autism classes used for community training activities. There were several fast-food restaurants, grocery stores, and small shopping malls near his school that were very welcoming and accommodating to students with autism. Parents of children with autism owned some of these stores. They would not only have been easier places to bring Justin, but their willingness to accommodate customers with autism made me want to be a regular customer as well.

✲ Lesson 3: There's safety in numbers

When we have difficulty handling the possible public reactions to our child, it helps to go out in pairs. Things that might worry or upset us when we have to deal with them alone can be less stressful when we have company. Sometimes these situations can even be funny.

Maureen

One day I was leaving an ice cream shop with five-year-old Justin firmly in hand and walking behind me. As I was chatting to my friend next to me, we were interrupted by a shriek of horror from a woman seated at the table nearby. As I turned and looked at her table, I saw Justin's hand holding two large scoops of her ice cream sundae, dripping ice cream, whipped cream, chocolate sauce, and nuts all over her table. If I had been alone, I would have wanted the earth to open up and swallow me. But because I was with a friend, I wanted to laugh. I tried to apologize while I desperately held back the waves of laughter. Between giggles, I think I offered to pay the woman for the sundae, but she was too stunned to respond. My friend and I got out of the shop and collapsed in hysterics while we tried to clean Justin up. I also made a mental note to myself, "Always walk with Justin in *front* of you in a store."

If you are a Superglue or Velcro personality when it comes to public outings, it can really help to hang around with Teflon people. Perhaps some of that ability to be unaffected by others' judgments or comments can rub off on us. We have a friend whose stories and storytelling ability make her one of the funniest "autism moms" we know. Putting a non-stick spin on the following story confirms in our minds that Terri is the Queen of the Teflon Personalities.

Terri

When Dallas was three and still nonverbal with a diagnosis of autism, I decided to take him to a new mall. We ended up in Sears. I had my 13-year-old son with us along with my nephew of the same age. The teenagers chatted along and talked in teenage lingo which I was just beginning to understand. ("Word" means "hello," "fat" means "good," "dawg" means "friend," etc.) As we were shopping, my son noticed that Dallas was missing. We didn't know our way around this new store, so we panicked and split up, running in different directions to look for him. My heart raced because I knew that he could not even tell anyone his name. I found the manager and he alerted security.

At last, the other boys came running up the escalator shouting that Dallas was downstairs. They also informed me that he had "taken a dump." It made me feel a little better to know that he was in the toy department playing with the trucks, as he had never paid attention to toys prior to this. This was a breakthrough! The boys ran ahead of me and we passed the toy department. No Dallas. They led me over to the plumbing section.

There in the middle of the plumbing section sat my baby boy on a display toilet with his disposable diaper dangling around his ankles. My heart raced, as this was the first sign ever that he was interested in toilet training. I was thrilled. Of course the boys were totally embarrassed as a crowd of onlookers gathered. The boys were even more "grossed out" (their words) when I helped Dallas down off the toilet and discovered he had had a bowel movement in the toilet. Dallas looked at me and said, "Dallas make do-do." This was the first time I had ever heard his voice. From the crowd, an angel of a man who wore wing tips and carried a very expensive briefcase handed me a monogrammed handkerchief to wipe Dallas. I proudly did so. What a glorious day!

The postscript to this story is that in the midst of this drama, Terri struck up a relationship with the store manager. She later introduced him to her cousin, whom he eventually married. (No, we are not making this up, we swear…)

✳ Lesson 4: It's okay to let someone else do it

Parents want their children with autism to be part of the community. But we are not the only ones capable of helping our children accomplish that goal. If the potential for public notice makes us anxious and uncomfortable, we can involve other people to help our children take advantage of community opportunities.

Maureen

From the time Justin was little, I wanted to give him every opportunity to enjoy recreational activities and practice living skills out in the community. The problem was I often felt anxious about his potential for disruptive behaviors in public. Then it occurred to me that I was not the only one capable of taking him to community activities. In fact my respite providers were usually less anxious and more adventuresome than I was. I would marvel at the places they took him: Sesame Street Live performances, church services, sit-down restaurants, crowded roller-skating rinks, and shopping malls. Justin usually rose to the occasion very well. Sometimes, I think Justin was affected by my anxiety about the potential for problems when we were in the community. His respite workers' relaxed and confident manners helped Justin to feel more relaxed and confident as well.

✳ Lesson 5: You may want to choose carefully how much information you give

Parents need to consider how to share information about their child with autism. Disclosure is not always an easy decision. Obviously, the professionals who will be working with your child need to know about the autism and your child's strengths and weaknesses. Those people who are going to develop a relationship with your child over a long period of time should know about the autism. But what about those individuals like the summer camp counselor, the substitute teacher, or the coach of the soccer team who may have only a short-term relationship with your child? Should they know about the diagnosis or have some understanding of your child's needs?

Parents also need to consider the people we come into contact with in the community – the neighbors, church or synagogue members, the barber, people in the grocery store or at the library, *et al*. How much do you tell them and how much can they understand? Having a child with unpredictable behaviors makes parents have to consider the "what ifs." What if, while your child is at the neighbor's house playing, he or she suddenly decides to run back home to get something and he or she doesn't know how to cross the street safely? Do you tell the neighbor about this possibility and what to do if it happens? What if your child has hearing sensitivities and can become upset by the loud music at church? Do you tell church officials or the people sitting around you that this might happen and why? It is complicated to know who to tell and how much to tell.

In her book *Pretending to be Normal*, Liane Holliday Willey discusses the issue of disclosure from the point of view of a parent who is also an individual on the autism spectrum. She suggests that we should think of people in two different groups: those who need to know and those who might not need to know about the diagnosis. Teachers, employers, coaches, and police officers would fall into the category of those who need to know. They need to know because they have authority over the individual's actions or their future. Disclosure is important when safety is an issue. Others who need to know would include people with whom the individual has a strong personal relationship such as close friends, relatives, roommates, co-workers, or romantic partners. Ms. Holliday Willey feels that physicians, counselors, or religious leaders would also fall into the category of those who need to know (Holliday Willey 1999).

It is important to realize that disclosure need not be a "tell all or tell nothing" situation. When we decide the swimming instructor needs to know more about our child, we don't have to tell him or her the definition of autism and the criteria for diagnosis. We can tell the instructor only that information that will help in working with our child. Maybe we tell the instructor that the child has some learning difficulties and may need some extra time to process the instructions. Maybe we share information about a sensory issue that may make our child overly sensitive to the feel of water on his face. It is possible and sometimes logical to disclose only the information that is needed, and not the diagnosis.

Ann

Over the years I have heard many different versions of how parents disclose information about their child to others. I liked the explanation from the mother originally from France who had moved to the U.S. when her child was very young. She would tell people her child was French and that's why he was acting differently. Or the mother who very calmly and without hesitation would say to people in the grocery store who were staring at her son, "He's retarded and that's why he acts this way." I was always somewhat shocked at her bluntness, but I admired her ability to be so honest.

My experience over the years is that you have to treat each situation individually. For each situation that comes up we have to gauge how important it is for the person to know, how much information he or she can handle or understand, and whether it will really help to disclose the information. I have always felt comfortable using the autism word to describe my son's difficulties to people who need to know. But not all parents feel the same way. Parents' willingness to disclose the diagnosis is always a very personal decision.

�֍ Lesson 6: Parents should respect the wishes of the individual with autism regarding disclosure

Some of our children are able to share their feelings about disclosure and some are not. When our children are very young or if they are not able to advocate for themselves, parents must make the decisions concerning who to tell and what to tell. However, as they age, some children can communicate their own opinions about disclosing. Many children with Asperger Syndrome or high-functioning autism are aware of their differences and may be sensitive to how others regard them. Making the decision to disclose or not should involve the child if he or she is able to participate in the decision.

An individual's decision to self-disclose is similar to the decisions we make as parents when our children are younger. Most parents struggle with who to tell about the diagnosis and how to tell them. Individuals with autism may struggle as well. We can help by discussing the different options with our children, sharing our advice, and encouraging them to share their own feelings about disclosing. The willingness of children on the spectrum to self-disclose will depend on how comfortable they feel about themselves and their autism or Asperger Syndrome.

This comfort level can be influenced by such factors as how long they have known about their differences and how long they have had an official diagnosis. How they learned about their disability and what experiences they have had in the past with their peers and with other people in the community can also be important factors. If children with autism do decide to disclose, we can help them choose the most comfortable way to share this information.

Ann

After finishing a semester in college in which Eric's grades were not as high as he would have liked, we discussed whether Eric should disclose about his autism to his professors. We were also concerned about a required course he was scheduled to take during the upcoming semester called "Interpersonal Communication," a course we knew would be very difficult for him. After we discussed the pros and cons of disclosing, Eric decided to let his professors know about his autism.

Eric was not comfortable with the idea of having to start a conversation with his professors about autism. He preferred to have something written that he could mail or hand to professors at the beginning of a semester. A therapist who works with Eric helped him draft his "Learning Guide." In this guide he states he has a learning disability called high-functioning autism and then describes how it affects his learning abilities. He describes his difficulty in taking tests, his difficulty with organizing himself and his materials, and his problems in distinguishing between relevant and irrelevant information in a lecture. He goes on to describe the strategies that he has found helpful, such as extended time on tests, hard copies of notes, and clear expectations for assignments. Eric also suggests that meeting with the professor periodically for feedback would be helpful. So far the responses from professors have been positive, and Eric is glad he decided to disclose in this manner (Palmer 2006).

Disclosure takes on a new dimension when we consider safety issues. Good relationships with first responders such as the police, emergency medical personnel, and fire fighters are crucial for keeping our children safe. But many behaviors and actions of individuals with autism are easily misunderstood, which can cause a tense situation to escalate. To avoid misunderstandings, parents should help their child have written or verbal ways to quickly provide information about their autism to the police or other emergency personnel.

✳ Lesson 7: Parents can help build allies in the public

There are more parents, professionals, and self-advocates working to raise public awareness of autism in our communities than ever before. Increasing the public's understanding and acceptance of individuals with autism should make it much easier for our children to succeed. It can also help to increase the support and resources our advocacy organizations need to serve all people on the autism spectrum. The following are some ways parents can help to make our communities more responsive to, and accepting of, individuals with autism.

(a) Encourage accurate, respectful media coverage that dispels myths and misconceptions about autism. Complain to the media when their coverage is not what it should be.

(b) Encourage our places of worship to welcome and accommodate people with autism into the life of their faith communities.

(c) Get involved in school and parent–teacher association initiatives that work to recognize and accept differences among people. Parents of typical kids and parents of children with autism share an interest in preventing bullying in school.

(d) Work to incorporate autism information into the training programs for law enforcement and emergency services personnel (Debbaudt 2002).

(e) Identify classmates or neighborhood peers who can serve as mentors for our children.

There are student leaders and athletes in our schools and neighborhoods who have the ability to influence how other students accept our children with autism. Among these students with influence are siblings of children with autism and children of autism professionals who are often willing to act as mentors. In one of our local high schools, a senior honors psychology class developed a student mentor program for students in their school with autism spectrum disorders (ASDs). This effort was led in part by a student whose mother is the executive director of the Autism Society of North Carolina. This group of mentors attended many school functions and participated in community activities either one-to-one with the student with ASD or in small groups. The program's success was enhanced by the fact that these students were among the leaders in the school.

❄ Lesson 8: Sometimes we assume people are judging our children when they are not

When parents feel vulnerable, we can be hypersensitive to criticism from others. Sometimes we read things into other people's reactions that are not what was intended at all. People's reactions may indicate surprise or curiosity rather than the disapproval or judgment we may imagine. Other people may actually want to help, but may be unsure how to do so.

Maureen

One day, while Patrick was in elementary school, after his doctor's appointment I suggested that we go out to lunch before I took him back to school. Alarmed, he said, "We can't! They will be wondering what I am doing at the restaurant instead of being at school." I asked him who "they" were, but I already knew the answer was "other people." I knew because "they" were in my head as well. "They" are the critical and judgmental Greek chorus of voices that I can project oh so easily onto the public around me.

When I was a young parent, I cared too much about other people's opinions. Perhaps I was still too close to my adolescent memories of how much the judgments of other people can hurt. Having experienced a few critical reactions toward Justin while in public, I took a giant leap and assumed everyone else would be critical as well.

Over the years, I have found the reactions of other people were often more sympathetic than critical. Many people were more ready to help than to judge. Perhaps the situations were easier for the public to understand as Justin got older because he appeared more obviously disabled as an adult than he had as a child. But I also got more comfortable just announcing Justin had autism and working to quickly de-escalate the incident. My focus on the task at hand left me little room to think about someone else's reaction. The good news about becoming an older parent is that your relationship with the public's reactions changes dramatically. In the book *Olivia Joules and the Overactive Imagination*, the heroine's favorite of her "Rules for Living" was a lesson I learned as I got older: Don't worry that people are thinking about you. They are actually focusing on themselves (Fielding 2003).

Ann

When I was at the parent orientation program at Eric's university, I was waiting in the student union on campus for a meeting to start. When I looked over the railing down to the lobby below, I saw a group of incoming freshmen waiting to go on a tour of the campus. I spotted Eric, but he did not see me. Eric was doing what he usually does when he is waiting; he was pacing and occasionally talking to himself, and every now and then he would bring his hand near his face and flick his fingers.

As I watched him with his college peers I realized how obviously different he looked. I was immediately concerned that the other students would know he was different and would not accept him. My overactive imagination had Eric ostracized, picked on, and made fun of, all the worst scenarios I could possibly imagine. Later, I could barely pay attention in the parent meeting because I was busy worrying about all the awful things that would happen to Eric.

The following morning, after Eric had spent the night in the dorm, my husband and I met him for breakfast. I was sure he would be unhappy or stressed about his first night at college. Much to our surprise, Eric was grinning from ear to ear when he greeted us at the door of his dorm room. He told us he had attended a social event for freshmen the night before, some sort of karaoke and dance event. Eric proudly showed us the water bottle with the school logo on it that he had won for being the "Best Male Dancer." I revealed my surprise and said, "Eric, I didn't even know you could dance!" Eric responded, "I didn't, either. I've never danced before in my life!" All my fears of ridicule from the other students were unfounded. Not only was he accepted by them but he was rewarded. I learned from this experience that sometimes my fears for Eric can lead me to misjudge how others might react (Palmer 2006).

Maureen

As we get to be middle-aged, we think about the losses that have started to accumulate – loss of parents, our empty nest, loss of our youthful appearance, and more. I approached middle age with the usual dread of body parts heading south and the sad realization that gravity was no longer my friend. But among all the losses you start to accrue with age, a wonderful loss is the gene that makes you care about what other people think. It's amazing to me now that my fear of the public's reaction to Justin was once so paralyzing and upsetting. Why I gave people I didn't even know the power to make me feel bad escapes me. I understand now what those with Teflon personalities have always understood: you consider the source and then move on. So if all else fails, and the strategies for dealing with people in the community do not diminish your anxieties about public notice of your child, there is one more consolation we can offer. Getting older is an effective cure for caring too much about the public's reactions to your child. Sometimes time really *does* heal some wounds.

Lessons for dealing with the public

1. It helps to find outings that work for the whole family.

2. You need to prepare for all contingencies.

3. There's safety in numbers.

4. It's okay to let someone else do it.

5. You may want to choose carefully how much information you give.

6. Parents should respect the wishes of the individual with autism regarding disclosure.

7. Parents can help build allies in the public:

   (a) Encourage accurate, respectful media coverage that dispels myths and misconceptions about autism

   (b) Encourage our places of worship to welcome and accommodate people with autism into the life of their faith communities

(c) Get involved in school and parent–teacher association initiatives that work to recognize and accept differences among people

(d) Work to incorporate autism information into the training programs for law enforcement and emergency services personnel

(e) Identify classmates or neighborhood peers who can serve as mentors for our children

8. Sometimes we assume people are judging our children when they are not.

Chapter 9

Accepting Our Children and Ourselves

"Acceptance" is an elusive concept with multiple meanings. In *A Difference in the Family*, Helen Featherstone identifies four different ways that parents may experience acceptance:

1. acknowledging the existence of the disability and its long-term significance

2. integrating the child and the disability into our lives

3. learning to forgive our own errors and shortcomings

4. searching for meaning in our loss.

(Featherstone 1980)

Since every parent of a child with autism has a unique interpretation of what acceptance means, all we can offer is our individual stories of what acceptance means to us – thus far.

❋ Lesson 1: Acknowledge the existence of the disability and its long-term significance

Maureen

Unlike many parents of children with autism, Rob and I knew from the time of Justin's birth that he was at risk for developmental delays. A lack of oxygen from his double-wrapped umbilical cord had caused Justin to develop seizures 12 hours after birth. Our training in child development immediately prompted concerns that his seizures would cause some degree of permanent brain damage and perhaps signal deeper underlying problems. Yet until his definitive diagnosis of chromosomal abnormality at age three, I clung to the hope that Justin's developmental problems would be mild and somehow correctable. As a pediatric nurse I had seen other children make remarkable recoveries from far more serious birth injuries than Justin's. But the diagnosis of his chromosomal abnormality ended my hope for a "miracle" recovery for Justin. As I read the only available medical article on partial trisomy #15, I understood that Justin's prognosis for normal functioning was grim. Reality had imposed profound limitations on his life and ours which I could no longer ignore.

However, as we adjusted to our collision with reality, there was also a certain freedom in knowing the limitations that the diagnosis presented. Understanding the long-term significance of profound mental retardation and severe autism was the first step in knowing what we were up against. As James Baldwin has said, "Not everything that is faced can be changed. But nothing can be changed until it is faced" (Baldwin 1998, p.54). Rob reminded me that the medical study I had read was not completely applicable to our lives. The study was based on a small sample of adults who lived in a state institution. Justin was a three-year-old child who had parents both willing and able to do everything possible to provide him with every advantage that special education could offer.

Rather than viewing acceptance as a passive surrender to fate, we tried to accept Justin's situation by actively moving on with our lives. This did not happen overnight. Within the limitations of his diagnosis and prognosis, we attempted to keep our expectations high enough to encourage progress, and realistic enough to avoid frustrating Justin or ourselves. That balance required constant readjustments over the course of his lifetime. My focus and energy went into finding ways to minimize autism's side effects and to maximize Justin's opportunities to learn and to live a quality life. He might never develop language, but we could teach him how to communicate. He would always need supervision and support, but we could surround him with people who would understand and care about him. He learned slowly and might never learn an entire job, but we could divide tasks into their smallest parts so he could master a few steps in the process. He struggled with disruptive and difficult behaviors, but we could provide medication and a structured environment that helped him to cope. He could not always show that he cared for us, but we could always show him how much we cared.

I have learned from Justin that living within limitations requires us to redefine success. As I look at Justin's psychological evaluations over the years, he has never tested beyond the functioning level of 24 months, whether the test was administered at age 2, age 10, or age 22. Yet when I consider his earlier prognosis and observe his present accomplishments, I believe he has surpassed expectations, surely one definition of success. As an adult he is still learning new skills and growing in independence.

Justin also helped me redefine what constitutes a quality life. Justin is deeply loved by his family. He lives in a place where people strive to understand, encourage, and care for him. He works where he is expected to contribute, but is not judged by his productivity. His life is filled with many activities that he finds pleasurable. From the time of his childhood when I despaired that he would never be happy, it is now more surprising to see him upset. Justin helped me to see that my vision of what constitutes a quality life was too narrow. Given his significant limitations, I really believe the quality of Justin's life is remarkable.

Ann

Unlike Maureen, I had no idea there was a problem until Eric was almost three years old. Even then the diagnosis of autism didn't provide us with many answers. It gave us a name for what we were facing but it didn't give us any information about what the future would hold for Eric or for our family. I desperately wanted to know what to expect, but no one was willing or able to predict the long-term significance of Eric's disability.

I tried to follow the advice of the professionals and focus on Eric's strengths. But recognizing his strengths was not always easy. The professionals were very encouraged by Eric's beginning language and his interest in books and letters and numbers. I wanted to be encouraged too, but at the same time I was receiving test results and reports that always emphasized how delayed Eric was. When I watched him with other children at preschool or at the park, his disability was even more obvious and it was difficult to feel optimistic. It was also impossible to feel positive about Eric's future when I was so overwhelmed with his frequent temper tantrums and rigid behavior.

At times my understanding of Eric's limitations and strengths and their significance would become clearer, but then something would happen that would make me question whether I really understood at all. Whenever Eric entered a new stage with new expectations I would have to reevaluate my beliefs about what his future would hold. His disability would either become more obvious or he would surprise me with what he was able to accomplish. For example, in the later years of elementary school and in middle school when social skills became more important, the gap between Eric and his peers widened. When the academic expectations of middle school became more challenging, his weakness in organizational skills became more apparent. At the same time he was surprising me with his flexibility and his ability to navigate a huge school campus, changing classes seven times a day. I never seemed to know how high to set my expectations for Eric and it complicated my acceptance of his disability.

Because the future is so unclear, it is difficult for parents of children like Eric to fully understand and accept the extent of the disability and its long-term significance. We can't know what to expect for the future because our children have major setbacks as well as periods of incredible growth. Making plans and decisions about the future is difficult when these children may not "fit" well into any program and finding appropriate services to meet their needs is so challenging.

When Eric was in high school, something happened that made me realize once again that I will probably never truly understand his disability and know what to expect. I had been away for a number of days on a business trip when I came home and asked Eric to come out of his room to greet me. When he came out, I said, "Hi Eric! Did you miss me?" He hesitated and didn't say anything. I felt sad for a moment that Eric doesn't show much affection towards me. I broke the silence and said, "That's okay, Eric. You don't have to answer." I walked away reminding myself that I know deep down he loves me, but he probably didn't miss me and that's okay. A few minutes later Eric came into my room where I was unpacking and said, "I didn't understand what you meant when you asked, 'Did you miss me?'" I explained to him that I was asking whether he thought about me while I was gone and whether he had realized that I wasn't there. He immediately answered, "Oh, yes, I missed you." It made me realize that, despite all his accomplishments, Eric continues to have difficulty understanding emotions and feelings. At the same time it was an incredible accomplishment for him to be able to read my facial expression for that brief moment, know that I felt sad, and want to make it better.

❊ Lesson 2: Integrate the child and the disability into family life

Maureen

Justin's needs have always taken center stage in our family drama. Our challenge was not how to integrate Justin into our lives, but how to extract some measure of "normal" family life while doing so. The persistent stumbling block to building a life after autism was the unpredictability and intensity of Justin's disruptive behavior. For many years our life revolved around preventing, managing, and recovering, both physically and emotionally, from his tantrums and meltdowns. When I was a new parent, these problems loomed larger than life. As I learned the lessons discussed in this book about balancing family life, advocating for Justin, taking care of myself, and trusting my instincts, life became somewhat more manageable. But even as I was gaining experience and knowledge, integrating Justin into our lives was a daily, often hourly, struggle. Eventually I found I needed more help than the lessons I learned on my own could provide.

My struggle was not so much with accepting Justin, but accepting that my life had turned out so differently from what I had expected. The metaphor for my early life with Justin is a tightly clenched fist with lots of white knuckles. Part of the time I was filled with a great anxiety. Life felt like it does when I am a passenger on an airplane, holding onto the armrest for dear life. I am fully convinced that it is my grasp, my concentration, and my will that is keeping the plane aloft. Justin's presence in our lives produced an unexpected flight plan, malfunctioning controls, and frequent, unpredictable turbulence. I knew if I loosened my grip on our lives, our family would certainly crash.

When my life was not clenched in a fist of anxiety, it was clenched in a fist of anger – at myself, Justin, Rob, the system, the world, the universe, and, ultimately, at God. I tried to ignore my anger by working harder to fix Justin and regain some control of my life. To my friends I appeared to be the proverbial duck on the pond that seems to glide effortlessly on top of the water. But underneath the surface I was furiously paddling just to stay afloat. With time I started to drown in the demands of Justin's caregiving and my responsibilities to the rest of my family. I felt more and more like everyone wanted a piece of me. I lost the energy required to contain my frustration, resentment, and anger over how difficult life had become. Rob finally said out loud what I knew deep inside: It was time for me to get some counseling.

In counseling I learned that the way to cope with my outer life was to take a long, hard look at my inner life. Counseling helped me recognize that somehow Justin's vulnerabilities had placed a tractor beam on my own, yanking them up to the surface. Talking things through with a counselor helped me connect some of the dots between my places of pain in the past and Justin's problems in the present. I realized how coping by staying insanely busy, taking on everyone else's responsibilities, avoiding conflict at all costs, and relying only on myself had helped me survive as a child. But as an adult, these ways of coping were not helping me accept my life and move on.

Counseling helped me unclench my anxious and angry grip on life. It allowed me to be more receptive to the support that was available to me.

One of the best sources of support became a 12-step program for Adult Children of Alcoholics (ACOA). While counseling gave me important insights into why my life felt so out of control, ACOA gave me a program for how to live.

I don't believe I have reached some settled or final stage of acceptance. What I have learned is that, in my life, acceptance will ebb and flow. Even now, when my life is so vastly improved from when Justin was first diagnosed, I have good days and bad days. I found a recent example in my remarks for a "Life after Autism" presentation that illustrates how my acceptance can vary depending on the day. The setting was a workshop for parents of younger children with autism. (It was the request for written information from those workshops that actually led to writing this book.)

I said:

> The first time I gave this talk I was in a great place. Justin was healthy and happy. His seizures, behaviors, and sensitive gut issues were all under control. He had made a good transition to a supported living arrangement with his care provider, who had been with him for over six years. I started to think we had arrived at a place where managing life after autism was no longer such a big deal. With my two "severely normal" children away at college, Rob and I were beginning to enjoy our empty nest. Today, only three weeks later, I am in a completely different place. Justin's gastrointestinal system is back in a mess. If I eliminate anything else as a potential food offender, his nutrition will consist of sucking air. His self-injurious behaviors are on the rise, along with my screaming at God, Justin, or anyone else in my path. His caregiver has suddenly and mysteriously quit and his living arrangement has fallen apart. Now I have to resume the hated task of finding and training new care providers. Starting this week, I am Justin's twice-a-day transportation to the farm where he works 45 minutes away. To top off my day, as I was driving to this presentation tonight, I got a call from home that Justin had just had a grand mal seizure.

Even now, my acceptance of Justin's place in my life remains a moving target. But most days I recognize that my life is what it is. I know that difficult days, while unwelcome, will not last forever. I can count on the return of the good days when things will go well.

Ann

I never felt driven to know why Eric had autism or what had happened to bring about this change in our lives. I only wanted to help Eric understand his world and be happy, and to make our family life easier. I expected the autism always to be a part of our lives, knowing and accepting that there was no cure but there were many ways to help. From the very beginning, the autism dominated our day-to-day activities and felt very integrated into everything our family did.

My acceptance of Eric's autism in our lives could have been even easier if I had learned earlier how my expectations for him were interfering with my understanding of him. I remember going to birthday parties of Eric's preschool classmates and seeing him playing by himself, ignoring the other kids, and covering his ears when they sang "Happy Birthday." It really hurt to see him looking so different from the other children. At some point, maybe when I was better able to accept his diagnosis, I realized that I was trying to fit Eric into a world that resembled my own world growing up, that was based on my own ideas of what was important in life.

I learned that when Eric is obviously having a difficult time in a situation, I should try to look at it from his perspective. Is this making Eric happy? Is this something he enjoys doing? Is this too difficult for him? And, the most important question, do I want him to do this because it is important to him or to me? Over the years, I've spent a lot of time grieving for what I thought were losses in Eric's life when in fact he was very happy and didn't seem to miss what I thought he was missing. I began to stop feeling so sad about how different his life is from what I expected and to be happy that Eric is happy, that he has a full life, and that he is loved by many people (Palmer 2006).

Reaching that point of acceptance is not an easy journey and is something all parents have to go through in their own way. Other parents and co-workers have asked me when I reached the point of accepting Eric for who he is. I don't remember having an epiphany one day when I suddenly could let go of the grief I felt about his disability. There were days when his disability didn't matter or I didn't think about it at all, and other days when I felt sad for what he didn't have in his life. It's not as if I was suddenly cured of the instinct to compare my child to others his age, or to feel pain when I thought of his future. Those feelings are definitely still there and rear their ugly heads at times totally out of my control. Maybe the point of acceptance for parents is simply the time we reach in our lives when the good feelings we have about our child occur more often than the bad feelings. The autism becomes only a part of our lives, one of many complications and features, and not the driving force.

For me acceptance does not mean accepting *where* my child is but *who* he is. There is a distinct difference. We should never be satisfied with where our children are in terms of their level of learning and their progress towards independence. We should never stop helping them achieve more because our children never stop learning. We have to raise the bar continually for our children. The acceptance I have strived for is more the acceptance of the uniqueness of my son than the acceptance of the limits on what he will be able to do.

Even though Eric's uniqueness may feel totally integrated and accepted into our family life most of the time, I know that there will always be times when my sadness about his autism will return, maybe just for a moment or maybe for longer. I was incapacitated by my grief those first weeks after hearing Eric's diagnosis. Though I never reached that same intense level of grieving again, at times over the years I have still been overwhelmed with sadness. Reminders of the experiences typical children go through may cause renewed pain: slumber parties, school field trips, the first date, turning 16, getting a driver's license, the prom. It's normal to feel sad if your child missed these milestones without the typical experiences we ourselves may have had. When this happens to me I remind myself that my son has his own achievements that are meaningful to his life and are worth celebrating too.

When Eric was in eighth grade, he said something that really put it all into perspective for me. All three of my children and I were sitting at the kitchen table. To start a fun conversation, I asked them, "If you had three wishes, what would you wish for?" Eric seemed to be having trouble thinking of something to wish for so I suggested, "What about a cure for autism?" Eric gave me a shocked look and said, "No, because then I couldn't do this!" and he flicked his fingers near his face, something he does when he is excited or happy. I realized at that point that he is very happy with who he is and that he wouldn't change anything about himself.

I recently discovered that my understanding of "who Eric is" can also change. I have always prided myself on being knowledgeable about autism and being the expert on my child. But I have learned recently that no matter how much I think I know my child and how his autism affects him, he can and probably will surprise me. Eric has always been socially withdrawn, preferring to be alone, and I thought he would be that way forever. Now he is surprising me every day with ways he is reaching out socially and the new interests he is developing as an adult. Seeing how he has changed, I have learned not to close any doors simply because I think my son won't go there (Palmer 2006).

The issue of accepting our children for who they are is an ongoing struggle for parents. When I think I totally respect and accept Eric for the individual he is, something happens to remind me that I need to continue to work on this. My mind tells me that Eric is great, for his wonderful sense of humor and personality, and for all of his strengths and unique attributes. I know I shouldn't care about those things that are different about his life. But my heart continues to be sad and afraid for him at times, even though he is not feeling these things about himself. Maybe this is a parent's burden to carry because of the depth of our love and connection to our children. I realize that I may never be completely satisfied with my son's life even though he may be very happy. I may accept the hand he has been dealt and the autism that has colored his life and my family's life. But I will probably never completely accept the fact that autism has complicated his life and added burdens that I wish I could remove.

✳ Lesson 3: Learn to forgive our own errors and shortcomings

Maureen

I approached my first 12-step meeting for Adult Children of Alcoholics with the same fear and discomfort I brought to my first "autism mothers" support group. I did not want to admit I fit the profile for membership in these particular clubs. But I gave it a try because the way I was managing my life was clearly not working. In both support groups I found that the opportunity to share personal experience, strength, and hope provided some serenity and greatly improved the quality of my life.

I felt lost before I started going to these meetings. I believed there was some single and perfect way to be Justin's mother, but due to some deficiency on my part, I had not been able to find it. Going to these meetings taught me many important lessons. I learned there was no one right way to be Justin's mother. I realized that my expectations for myself were impossibly high. I learned that, while raising a difficult child, all I could do was the best that I could on any particular day. That meant some days would be better than others. I was not perfect and that was okay. The goal became progress, not perfection. I surrendered much of the worry that my flaws and my lack of perfection would adversely affect my family. I came to see that we were all much more resilient than I had imagined.

Ann

It may be easier to learn to live with autism than it is to learn to live with ourselves. There is an interesting exercise we do as part of the training for the volunteer parent mentor program that I coordinate. We separate into small groups and take turns talking about the strengths and abilities we have developed as a result of parenting a child with autism. Most of us participating in this training have difficulty complimenting ourselves, especially regarding our abilities as parents.

I especially struggle with this exercise. As I have mentioned before, I have rarely felt confident in the parenting decisions I have made over the years concerning Eric. There never seemed to be obvious "right" answers; everything was always a guess. Then I always had mixed emotions about the choices I made. Should I have pushed him more? Would Eric be doing better if I had tried that therapy? Was it a mistake to make him participate in that program? Part of my learning to accept myself has come from understanding that the choices I have made were the best I could make at the time for Eric and for our family. I see other parents also making tough decisions and choices, some of which I don't necessarily agree with and would not choose for my own son. It helps me accept my own shortcomings when I see that I am not alone and that others are also taking risks, making difficult choices, and just doing what they think is best for their own families.

I have learned a great deal over the years about my own strengths and weaknesses. I realize now that I can't do it all, that I can't remove my emotions from all the decisions I make as a parent, and that I can't live Eric's life for him (as much as I would like to). There are always going to be aspects of my personality that influence what I can or can't handle and what I am able to do as Eric's mother. I have learned to forgive myself for what I may have done wrong over the years and tried to chalk up those mistakes as "learning experiences." I also forgive myself for not being all that I imagine a perfect mom should be.

Many families face more difficult challenges with autism than I have personally experienced. I have deep respect for parents who struggle daily with severe behavioral, medical, or self-care issues that I have miraculously escaped. When Eric's behaviors improved and our life became much calmer, I would occasionally feel almost guilty about how well Eric was doing. At parent support meetings I often didn't feel as though I had any right to complain or even contribute to the conversation when so many around me were dealing with harder situations. Our challenges with Eric over the years seemed trivial compared to the stories of others. As much as I wanted to be a part of the collective suffering of the autism community, I sometimes felt like an outsider.

I don't feel like an outsider anymore. It has taken me years to stop feeling this guilt and to accept and understand my contributions to the autism community. I know now that my experiences are meaningful, although different from those of some others. Each of us, no matter where our child is on the spectrum or what daily issues we face, has had struggles, and we all deserve support and a feeling of belonging. We can't possibly compare such diverse issues as toilet training a young adult with autism and mental retardation to helping a teenager with Asperger

Syndrome understand why he doesn't have any friends. Each situation is difficult. We are all dealing with challenges and can benefit from the support of others who share our pain, even though they may not have shared our particular experiences. So I have learned over the years that it is okay that our children have different challenges and different successes. Our lives cannot be compared on some instrument that measures "who has it worse."

My insecurities and doubts are gradually being replaced by greater confidence in myself as Eric's mother. I have learned through my mistakes and stressful experiences and I can now make better choices and deal with difficult situations more easily than when I was younger. But I also know that I will continue to make mistakes, to misjudge Eric sometimes, and to question my decisions and actions.

❋ Lesson 4: Search for meaning in our loss

Maureen

My initial impulse to get involved in relationships with other parents of children with autism was driven by self-interest. I needed both information and support to help me manage my life. I also knew Justin and our family would benefit from involvement with advocacy organizations that worked on behalf of people with autism. But my advocacy work and relationships with other parents came to mean much more to me than any immediate advantages I received from them. The opportunity to witness such unselfish acts of love, courage, and sacrifice that parents perform every day heartened me. The many ways I was helped by other parents made me want to help someone else. As I grew in my ability to help other parents, I felt better about my own life.

Finding meaning in my relationships with other parents was easy. Finding meaning in my spiritual life proved a much harder search. It began on the day that Justin was diagnosed.

Rob recognized that very day the challenge to faith that a child with disabilities presents. We left the Developmental Evaluation Center trying to make sense of what we had just been told. In the midst of our conversation, Rob said, "You know, this diagnosis raises essentially spiritual questions." I thought, "What in the world are you talking about?" My mind was spinning on everything else but spiritual matters. So I paid little attention to what he had said and attributed his remark to the musings of someone who had been a philosophy major in college.

But Rob was right. Whenever we search for meaning in the events of our lives we are asking essentially spiritual questions. Having a child with disabilities engages us up close and personal with the great questions of life. What makes life worth living? What is the meaning of life? How is it that an all-powerful and all-loving God allows terrible things to happen to people? Why did this happen to us?

In over 25 years of relationships with other parents, these questions have rarely been discussed. We have revealed to each other some of the most intimate and difficult problems of our lives, yet I have rarely been in a discussion about how our child with autism has affected our faith. I find that I am hesitant to bring this subject up even now. Like many others, I have experienced the reality that differences over spiritual beliefs can divide and discomfort us rather than unite and console us. After Justin's diagnosis, I remember how angry and alone I felt when other people gave me unsolicited, glib reassurances about God's role in my life. They would say, "God is in control of the world" and I would think, "Yeah, well He is doing a lousy job." Or "God never gives you more than you can handle" and I would think, "Well, He comes pretty damn close." Or "God's ways are not our ways" and I would think, "When it comes to Justin, my ways would have been a whole lot better."

It was this last question that bothered me the most. I have many references to my struggles with God's role in Justin's life throughout my journals: "Is He watching over us at all?" "Is there a plan for Justin's life that does not condemn him to a life of confusion and self-injury, ultimately forcing us to place him away from his family?" "God would not have created Justin only to abandon him. But where is He…?" It was my feeling of being abandoned that made me slam the door to an already tenuous relationship with God. I was in a special kind of hell watching Justin hurt. For the next ten years, Justin's presence in my life was proof positive that God did not care or intervene in the affairs of the world. My parting remark directed to God was "You may have abandoned this child, but I will not." Inwardly, an attitude was forged that said "It is Justin and me against the world." I decided to rely on myself and take over without God. I managed this way for about ten years because my self-sufficiency was pretty strong. But eventually life overwhelmed my resilience as I gradually discovered I could bend the realities of my life to my will only so far.

My tipping point towards a different view of my faith came during a walk when Justin was about ten years old. It was a terrible day when I was at my emotional endpoint and Justin was relentlessly tantruming. I found a deserted piece of a county park where we could walk and I could let him scream his head off. I had gotten into the 12-step program and was "working the steps." I had taken the first step before my first meeting.

I had no problem freely admitting, "my life had become unmanageable." I had progressed through the second step, which was to accept that there was a greater power than myself that could restore me to sanity. But I was stuck on the third step that required I make a decision to turn my life and my will over to the care and keeping of a Higher Power (however I define Higher Power). In the park I was thinking about the third step. I started to feel my anger rise. All the questions I had raised and then buried from my journal boiled up to the surface. To stop the flow of my anger would be like trying to cap a volcano with a garbage-can lid. Kathleen Norris says "that sometimes the power to name, to describe, and to lament is the only power we have" (Norris 1997, p.xiii).

I left the park that day with no miracle answers. Initially, I felt better only because I was empty and drained. Yet somehow, imperceptibly, I had opened some kind of door to explore more about the spiritual questions in my life. By confronting my anger at the unfairness of life, I felt a sense of release. I became intrigued about how other people dealt with the questions of suffering and faith. At first I found some books and what I read spoke to my doubts. Later on I found a support group that would help me take on my questions of faith. After 15 years of meeting with these friends to confront my spiritual questions, I still have not found completely satisfactory answers. But I am also no longer doing my best imitation of Mt. St. Helen's.

My experience confirms what much wiser people have concluded throughout the ages. The greatest single problem of religious faith is the presence of unwanted, undeserved, and unexplainable suffering. Frederick Buechner writes that:

> The world hides God from us, or we hide ourselves from God, or for reasons of his own, God hides himself from us, but however you account for it, he is often more conspicuous by his absence than by his presence. (Buechner 1977, p.43)

My experience of God's absence after Justin's diagnosis is what launched my spiritual search. Since then my feelings about my life and my faith have changed. I no longer debate all the questions of life expecting to find all the answers. I realize that there are mysteries about how God works in the world that I will never understand, or even fully accept. Yet I have found some peace in the two spiritual truths that I once heard in a sermon: "There is a God and I'm not Him."

In the meantime I have decided to give God the benefit of my doubts. Harold Kushner says, "people crave consolation more than explanation" (Kushner 2003, p.106). My spiritual beliefs now console me. So does the presence of the amazing people who have come into my life in ways that I no longer believe is mere coincidence. First among those people is Justin. A friend once told me that God is found in the interruptions of life. Justin provided an interruption *extraordinaire*. He has forced me to live a life full of paradox. How did one of the hardest relationships in my life lead me to take action and change my behavior in ways that have made my life so much easier? Would I have gone where I needed to go without the extra demands that Justin brought into my life?

From a time when I believed Justin was evidence of God's absence in my life, I now believe Justin is incontrovertible evidence of God's presence. He is a blessing in my life, though not in the sickly sweet, sentimentalized cliché that people offer when they say special children are a blessing from God. Justin was a wake-up call type of blessing. In requiring me to fight long and hard to make sense of my life, I feel a kinship with Job and the writers of the Psalms. Justin has been the fierce blessing that Aeschylus describes:

> He who learns must suffer. And even in our sleep, pain that cannot forget falls drop by drop upon the heart, and in our own despair, against our will, comes wisdom to us by the awful grace of God. (Bartlett 1992, p.63)

Ann

The pain I felt when Eric was first diagnosed is hard to remember now. That deep feeling of loss is not there anymore. How can having Eric in my life be a loss? Loving him has enriched my life in many ways. He is constantly teaching me new ways to look at things. His brutal honesty and innocence reminds me of how superficial people can be, and what is important in life (and what isn't). He has taught me to judge people less and accept people more. I have a much deeper appreciation of all people who are different, not only people with disabilities, but people who make different life choices or have different beliefs from my own.

Having a child with autism has taught me that I can find celebrations even in difficult situations. When Eric recently lost the key to his dorm room it was stressful for him and turned out to be an expensive mistake. But I was so happy that Eric could independently report it to the right people and successfully take care of getting the lock changed. When he was in high school and came home from school one day and reported that he had gone to the wrong classroom, I was not upset that he had gotten lost. I was happy that instead of my "interrogating" him that day, he willingly initiated telling me about something important that had happened to him. I've learned that the seemingly difficult situations often are trivial in the big picture of things, and there are frequently positive outcomes we don't expect.

Having a child who has struggled at times has also helped me appreciate more the accomplishments of my other children. It was exciting to witness the learning that came so naturally to them when they were toddlers. Their curiosity about the world, the speed with which they learned, their ability to watch and imitate others: these were all reasons for celebration. And now, as they have gotten older, it is not their academic abilities that impress me so much as their abilities to develop relationships and solve problems. These are skills that I appreciate because I know how difficult they are for individuals with autism like Eric. My daughter is leaving soon to study abroad for four months and I am reminded again of the skills required for her to do this. I am sad about her leaving, but I am impressed by her courage to go somewhere far from home where she has never been, where she doesn't know anyone, and where they will be speaking a language that will take work for her to understand. It makes me very proud to consider all she has accomplished to be able to take this important step in her life.

Eric's diagnosis has also brought many interesting, passionate people into my life; people I would never have met otherwise. I am constantly inspired by the parents, professionals, and individuals with autism whom I meet. I have been fortunate to develop wonderful friendships through my contacts in the autism community. These friendships, along with all that Eric has taught me and all I have learned about myself and about life, have given me much more than I have lost.

Parenting Eric has also led me to career choices I would not have made if autism had not been a part of my life. My work with families of individuals with autism is more meaningful and fulfilling than anything else I have done in my life. After years of needing support and help from others, I am now able to give something back to help families that are going through similarly difficult times. Having that opportunity is a gift I am very thankful for.

Lessons for accepting our children and ourselves

1. Acknowledge the existence of the disability and its long-term significance.

2. Integrate the child and the disability into family life.

3. Learn to forgive our own errors and shortcomings.

4. Search for meaning in our loss.

Chapter 10

Letting Go
Ann's Story

Eric's transition to college life was both difficult and exciting. I had very mixed emotions: one minute feeling happy and proud of all he had accomplished, the next minute being scared and unsure about whether he would be able to handle the responsibilities of being a college student. Some of the transition process, which I describe below, is covered in greater depth in my book *Realizing the College Dream with Autism or Asperger Syndrome: A Parent's Guide to Student Success* (Palmer 2006).

We spend years gradually letting go of our children. When they are toddlers we begin letting them walk a little bit ahead of us. Then we stand back and hold our breaths as we watch them explore the climbing apparatus on the playground. We are still on "parent alert," but we begin to understand that they can and should do things without us. We are traumatized when we leave them crying at preschool the first time. But that becomes a distant memory as they barely acknowledge us when they walk confidently into their elementary school. As adolescents our children begin pushing us away in their urgency to discover who they are. And by high school they often have made our lives so difficult that the thought of them leaving home seems too good to be true.

The process of letting go is quite different for parents when their child has a disability. Those early stages of letting our children gradually leave our side to explore the world are especially tough when the child is a child with autism. Our children's vulnerability and unpredictable behaviors can make us especially protective and fearful. It requires courage to let our children take chances and move towards being more independent. As our children become adults, reality requires that we encourage them to move beyond the protective boundaries we have so carefully placed around them.

The gradual stages of letting go that I have experienced with all three of my children were very different with Eric. Eric wasn't as eager to explore on his own and be independent. He always needed encouragement to try anything new. He never showed the defiant and rebellious attitude of an adolescent. Many of the same fears I felt as Eric began exploring the playground were present when he walked into a new school or a new classroom. Those same fears were magnified when I left him alone in his college room. In each situation, no matter what his age, I was afraid that he would get hurt, or fail, or that someone would take advantage of him.

One thing that has helped lessen my fears has been educating myself about services and supports available for Eric. Increasing my knowledge has helped me feel less confused and more confident. Just as when Eric was first diagnosed, there was more information about services than I could possibly absorb. Once again I was overwhelmed by what I didn't know and needed to know in order to help my son. There were new acronyms to learn and new agencies and people to contact. I needed to learn about social security, vocational rehabilitation, residential and day program options, and supported employment services. It was an incredible amount of information to take in and a mountain of paperwork to complete.

I also had to research what options were available for Eric at the college level. When I began reading and searching the internet, I was amazed at the variety of options that are available for students. I learned about community colleges and technical schools, online courses and video courses, commuting to college and residential options. I looked carefully at the colleges and universities in my area, what the services for persons with disabilities were like at each institution, and which colleges had served students on the spectrum before.

As I did almost 20 years ago when Eric was first diagnosed, I reached out to other parents who had been through this transition before me. Their advice and guidance helped me survive the stress of this process. I also reached out to trusted professionals who knew Eric and could advise me about what we needed to do to make this transition successful. Finding people who could help Eric (and me!) has made me feel more supported through this challenge.

Unlike when Eric was three and I was navigating the world of special education and disabilities services by myself, this time Eric had to be involved in the learning process with me. He needed to learn what resources were available and how to access them. He had to understand his choices and know how to advocate for himself as an adult. I knew college would give him experience in practicing these important self-advocacy skills.

When we received notice that Eric had officially been accepted into college, we were ecstatic. When the excitement wore off a little, I suddenly realized that I had about three months to teach Eric everything he needed to know about life. This transition to leaving home was going to be the hardest thing Eric had ever done, and a real test of his ability to survive and take care of himself. I felt more confident in his academic abilities and much less confident in his functional skills, those he would need to take care of himself. I knew that there were areas of daily living that Eric was not prepared to carry out independently.

When I realized how much Eric needed to learn before going to college, I knew I had to find a way to help him prepare without driving him crazy. Eric is not fond of spontaneous, lengthy conversations and I knew he wouldn't want to be talked to all summer about preparing for college. My solution was to schedule "meetings" with him to talk about issues related to college. Eric could see on the calendar when we would meet. I let him know before each meeting what we would be talking about so he could think about the topic and come up with any questions he might have.

We met weekly during the summer before his first year in college. Topics of our discussions included safety (how to stay safe on campus and in his room), health issues (how to know when he is sick and who to go see), self-help (hygiene, laundry, money management), and time management (how to decide when to study and when to play and what to do during his free time). We also met and talked about academic strategies, such as how to know when he needed help and whom to seek out. We talked about taking notes during lectures, studying for exams, and how to break up a writing project into smaller steps. These meetings were very helpful, not only to prepare Eric for what he would need to do but also to prepare me for letting him go. I gained more confidence in his ability to take care of himself as he learned more about what would be expected of him in college.

What a student needs to learn before transitioning to college is going to vary. Some students will need more preparation in financial matters, while others may need help with hygiene or health issues. The student's strengths and challenges should determine the areas to be addressed. I tried to imagine what a day in a college student's life is like, then tried to picture Eric dealing with those same issues. What would be easy for him and what would make him anxious?

The orientation at Eric's university was very helpful in our preparations for college. Eric attended a two-day orientation for incoming freshmen while my husband and I attended the orientation meetings for parents. We received information about how to access services at the university and about the day-to-day expectations for students. It helped me to see that the other parents attending the orientation were also feeling scared and anxious about their children leaving home.

The orientation gave Eric the opportunity to spend his first night in a college dormitory and to meet other incoming students. He was able to talk with his academic advisor for the first time and sign up for his first semester classes with the advisor's help. Eric was able to hear from older students about their first year in college, what was hard and what was fun, and how they felt about leaving home. All of these experiences helped Eric feel more comfortable about what was to come.

The day we moved Eric into the dormitory was extremely hard for me. I was an emotional wreck inside. I wanted to be strong and share in his excitement, and I managed to hold it together until the drive home. As soon as I was alone with my husband in the car, the floodgates opened and I cried the entire drive home. It was a gloomy, rainy day. As I was looking out the window I was reminded of another rainy day 16 years earlier when I was also crying in the car. That rainy day, my husband and I were driving home after just receiving Eric's diagnosis of autism. That day I was crying for the fear I felt for Eric and for the uncertainty of his future. I was crying for the loss of the dreams I had for my son. As we were driving home from leaving Eric at college, my tears were again partially because I was afraid for Eric. I wasn't sure whether the other students would accept him or whether he would be safe living on his own. But this time the tears weren't because of a loss of the dreams we had for Eric. My tears were in celebration of the new dreams we had for him and how far he had come since the day he was diagnosed with autism.

Maybe the chapter title "Letting Go" does not accurately describe what I have experienced through this transition with Eric. It should probably read "Beginning the Letting Go Process." I am still very involved in Eric's life. I am not making the decisions for him anymore, but I advise him and he continues to come to me for help. I think of my friends, such as Maureen, who have transitioned their children into residential living situations. They have transferred many of the day-to-day parenting responsibilities to someone else. This must be a difficult experience for any parent. In my situation with Eric, I have transferred some of my parenting responsibilities to Eric himself, rather than to someone else. In many ways it is similar to what I am also experiencing with my daughter, as she is growing up and needing me less.

However, Eric will probably always need me or another person in his life to provide some level of support. I can't predict at this point how much support he will need, but I am prepared to help him in any way I can. I know that I can't (and shouldn't) carry that burden of responsibility indefinitely, so I will continue to focus on helping him become as independent as possible. With the help of the career counseling office on campus, Eric will begin the process of developing his resumé, learning to do interviews, and, eventually, finding meaningful employment (I hope!). When that happens, we will enter the next stage of letting go.

It seems natural to me that Eric and I have reached this point in our lives. I am almost 50 years old; it is a time when my children are getting older and moving on with their lives. It is a time for me to start looking ahead to the days of less childrearing and having more time for myself and my husband. Intellectually I know it is the normal progression of things, but it still hurts. Eric has needed me and I have needed him for a long time. It is hard not having that intense, daily connection anymore.

Eric's life may be different from the one I originally envisioned for him before he was diagnosed. But since his diagnosis, his life is better and his future more promising than anything I could have imagined for him. I believe that most of us who have parented children with autism want the same things for our children's future. We want them to be safe and happy. We want them to have a full life and be surrounded by people who care about them. Letting go and allowing them to take risks and explore without us is a necessary part of our children's journey to reach the life we want for them. As difficult and scary as it may be, letting them go is a part of loving them. For lessons in learning about letting go, see the box at the end of Chapter 11.

Chapter 11

Letting Go
Maureen's Story

My mom once confided in me why she thought parenthood was the most difficult job in the world. Parents invest years of love, hard work, and sacrifice to help their children become independent. If they are successful, they work themselves out of a job. I became acutely aware of this planned obsolescence of parenthood when Michael and Patrick started high school. As I imagined them leaving for college, I grieved over letting them go. By senior year in high school they had been tugging at that emotional umbilical cord for quite a while, pushing away towards greater independence. They were so excited and so ready to leave that it was hard not to feel the same way. Of course, their typical teenage behavior was nature's way of advising Rob and me that an empty nest might not be such a bad thing after all.

I never expected to feel ready for Justin to leave home in this way. Rob and I talked about some hypothetical day in the future when Justin would move from our home to a quality group home in our community. But I never believed I would feel it was the right time for Justin to move. Although I knew Justin could not live with us forever, I was overwhelmed at the prospect of having him live anywhere else. I believed that I was the only one willing and able to care for him. I was the expert: his best teacher, case manager, and most effective advocate all rolled into one. I felt trapped in a Catch-22: Justin could not live with us forever, but he couldn't live without us. I was only half-joking when I said that the only solution I could see to guarantee Justin's future was for me to neve die.

Throughout Justin's elementary school years I stayed at the periphery of the world of adult services for people with autism. I was too preoccupied with Justin's present needs and the future looked too scary to dwell on for very long. By the time Justin entered high school, however, that future I had avoided was rapidly coming into view. I decided to become more proactive about his transition to life after high school. To guarantee Justin's future, my Plan A was still to live forever, but I decided I needed a Plan B just in case.

Transition services designed to help students move from public school to post-school activities had recently been mandated, but were not sufficiently developed to meet Justin's needs. So, I began to explore the world of adult services through the same channels I had used in the past. The people I used to jump-start my education were parents who had adult children with autism and the professionals I respected in the schools, in private practice, and in advocacy organizations. They helped me identify the two major tasks to prepare for Justin's transition. The first task was to decide what kind of living and working environment we wanted for Justin. The second task was to explore the world of adult services to find which programs might be a good match.

Justin had six years remaining in his mandated school education. Rob and I spent some time getting more specific about what we wanted for Justin after his high school years ended at age 21. In our planning we tried to include what we believed Justin would want if he were able to tell us. We came up with the following list: That he would be safe; that he would be happy; that he would be surrounded by people who understood him, liked him, and would appreciate what he had to offer; that he would have choices; that he would be allowed to have good days and bad days; that he would be encouraged to learn new skills and grow in independence; that he would not hurt himself or others; that he would live in our community, but not in our house; that he would participate in community life; that parent involvement would be valued wherever he lived or worked; that he would live in a place that felt like home; that his transition from home to job would be seamless; and that he would have an "enviable life" (Guthrie Medlen 2004, p.2).

Our dreams for Justin were not totally new. They were variations on the same themes that had guided our IEP planning each year. Our dreams had been gradually tempered by certain realities regarding the severity of his level of autism and mental retardation. They had evolved as I grew to know Justin better and understand more about his strengths, his interests, and his needs.

When Justin was in high school, we had the opportunity to visit a residential farm program in a nearby community. We decided this kind of farm program played to Justin's interests and strengths. Since he was little, he had always liked being outdoors, taking special delight in water and wind. Throughout his childhood, he liked to hike on nature trails where he could crunch or kick the fallen leaves. This was his tree hugger stage; as we hiked, he would stop and embrace the trunk of a tree. Now his favorite recreational interests were still outdoor activities such as hiking, swimming, and skating. We also considered that the jobs on a farm would play to his strengths with gross motor activities such as moving, lifting, watering, and carrying. Manual labor and the opportunity to get up and move around between jobs help Justin prevent and manage his disruptive behaviors. More complicated farm chores could be divided into smaller tasks so Justin could contribute to some part of the chore. A farm also provided some of the variety in jobs that Justin would prefer over repeating the same task for long periods of time. On a farm Justin would have enough space that he would not have to work next to people in close quarters. But he would still have the chance to indulge his social side when he was in the mood. In the outdoors he would not disturb other people when he was loud, which can occur when he is happy and when he is upset. (Though I suspect that his noisy nature has more to do with his inherited family traits than with his autism.) Finally, Justin can be fairly flexible about changes in routine, which would be an asset in an environment so influenced by unpredictable events such as changes in weather.

Whatever future residential and vocational setting we found for Justin would also have to address his needs. To be safe, he would require close supervision because he has little understanding of danger. He would need assistance to complete many of the activities of daily living and of his job. He would require a staff that was understanding, well trained, and supervised. His program would have to value parental involvement.

Once we had defined the type of program we believed would best serve Justin after high school, we changed how we approached his IEP planning. When he was younger we had elaborate IEPs full of goals for every possible skill he might need in order to function in the world. But by the time he reached adolescence, we chose to work more intensively on those specific goals and activities that would help him with life after high school. So we dropped some goals and made new priorities. The skills we decided to work on at home and at school became expanding his object schedule, self-care and hygiene, toileting, cooking, household chores, and outdoor yard work.

As we worked on Justin's transition from school, I began to explore what services were available for adults with autism. I visited programs in my community and some located in other parts of the state and outside of North Carolina. I wanted to learn about best practices, and was disturbed to find out that there were not many out there.

I was stunned by how fragmented, complicated, and confusing the world of adult services could be. To this day I am not sure I have been able to figure the whole system out. There were critical shortages and long waiting lists for quality programs. Because adult services are not mandated, Justin might be deemed eligible for a program but not be guaranteed a place. There was inadequate funding for available programs and no long-range planning or funding in sight. The lack of coordination between the various agencies serving adults was startling. Getting the different agencies to work together appeared to be like herding cats. I knew getting a program in place for Justin would require a commitment of hard work and creativity that would exceed any advocacy efforts I had made in the past.

There were two additional problems in gearing up to advocate for Justin's transition. The first problem was that I was ready to gear down. My energy and tolerance for advocacy were waning. I was tired of the explaining, defending, promoting, and interpreting I had done for him over the years. I had developed the skill set and the support system to be an effective advocate, but I was less willing. I had greater knowledge, but a much shorter fuse for ineffective, inefficient people and systems. I wanted someone else to "get it" and just make things happen for my son. My second problem was that Justin still lived at home. His adolescence was difficult and getting him through the day was a full-time job. I felt incredible tension between the present demands and all this future planning. I knew if something became available, I would need to grab it even if I was not really ready for Justin to leave home.

This was the case when Justin turned 18. The residential farm program, the Carolina Living and Learning Center (CLLC), opened its last home and we decided to apply. I knew and respected the professionals involved and was impressed with the program. I knew the farm would be a perfect fit for Justin. It passed my test of whether it was the kind of place that I would want to live in myself. But although Justin was appropriate for the program, so were many, many others. He made it to the final cut, but someone else was accepted because that individual and his family's need for services exceeded our own.

The year we applied to the CLLC was a very difficult one. While waiting for the placement decision, I seemed to change my mind almost daily about what I wanted that decision to be. One day I felt as though I would die if Justin were accepted. The next day I felt like I would die if he were denied. When Justin was not accepted, part of me understood why the admission committee made that decision. I was acquainted with many of the other applicants and many of them were in great need. I had no question that the committee had agonized over their difficult placement decisions. Since they knew our family, it had to be particularly painful for them to turn Justin down. But in my heart, for at least the next year, it felt quite different. It felt as if Justin were being rejected because he wasn't judged to be good enough. He had lost the autism version of a beauty contest because he didn't quite measure up. I felt even more distressed when I considered that, if this program could not find a place for Justin, how could anyplace else?

While the door to residential services at the CLLC closed, a door opened for Justin to work at the farm during the day. This is the farm where he worked with his aide, Robin, during his last three years of high school. When Justin graduated from high school at age 21, Robin resigned from the school system and became his full-time job coach at the farm. Justin and Robin worked together at the farm for three additional years. During this time, Robin approached me about creating a supported living arrangement for Justin in her home. Justin and Robin were very fond of each other. She had seen him through one of the roughest stretches of his life. She had done overnight respite care for Justin at her house, and he already considered her house a second home.

We decided to give it a try. For about a year our supported living arrangement worked pretty well. Justin lived at her house for about four days a week and transitioned easily between our house and hers. But cost became an issue as we tried to upfit Robin's house to meet all the supported living regulations. Justin's Medicaid waiver did not provide sufficient funds to cover his 24-hour-per-day supervision needs. Other issues arose and ultimately it became clear that we had different visions for how to proceed with this supported living arrangement. Robin resigned rather suddenly and we brought Justin back home.

It took time and some grieving to get over losing Robin and this opportunity for Justin. But I learned an important lesson. Robin's home had been an appealing model because it gave Justin a very homelike setting. But for his safety and security over the course of his adult life, I wanted him connected to the resources of a larger organization and not to just one person.

When Justin came home I returned to my status as full-time caregiver and chauffeur. I was lucky to recruit back some former caregivers to help. They started to kid me about how laid back I had become about working on Justin's goals. They shared their surprise at seeing me ignore Justin's schedule in favor of a walk in the park or just hanging out. They pointed out that I was doing things for Justin with self-care and chores that he was capable of doing for himself. Their teasing made me realize that over the last year, I had gone through a transition myself. I had reached the point where I no longer wanted to be the person who pushed Justin to be independent and learn new skills. I had grown tired of being his teacher, case manager, and advocate rolled into one. I wanted someone else to assume those roles and let me just be his mom.

Once I realized that other people were doing a better job with Justin than I was, I knew it was time for Justin to leave home. I knew in my heart no one could love him more, but other people could now offer him more. If he stayed home, at the rate I was going, he would start losing opportunities rather than gaining them. My feelings were remarkably similar to those I felt when Michael and Patrick left for school. It was time. We were ready for a new relationship. *If* I could find a place that was a good fit, it would be better for Justin to leave home.

Then the big *if* revealed itself. The former and current directors of the CLLC knew Justin was thriving in a farm setting. They made me aware that another agency was collaborating with them to build a similar residential farm program in our state. Ironically, I had been tangentially involved in the public hearings that approved this new farm program when I had been asked by an advocacy organization to speak about the need for residential options. I had known at the time it would be a good program under an agency that was highly regarded for its quality work in the field. I never pursued this farm program, however, because it was two hours away from my home. But now two hours away did not seem so far, as I was driving more than two hours a day to transport Justin to work at the CLLC. So, intrigued by the possibility and aware that opportunities were few and far between, I decided to go visit.

When I went to meet with the executive director, I had a list of questions a mile long. About ten minutes into our lunch, I gently laid them aside. There was an immediate fit between what I had heard about the program, what she told me about their plans, and how it felt in my gut. I recognized that this was the program for Justin. I knew that all my questions, as well as the ones I had not thought to ask, would be answered to my satisfaction before the day ended.

We applied to Carolina Farms and Justin was accepted. Throughout the process, I made a conscious decision to put my emotions on hold. I needed to deal with many practical and time-consuming preparations. I worried that if I let my emotional guard down I would not get everything done. Besides, I thought to myself, who knows how I will feel when the day comes for Justin to leave? I decided to try to wait and deal with my feelings then.

The day we took Justin to the farm, Rob and I sobbed in the car all the way home. It was the most bittersweet day of my life. We discussed our journey with Justin from the two clueless kids who thought his presence was such a loss to the middle-aged parents who were now overcome with grief at his leaving their home. It was a difficult, important, and healing conversation. When we were younger, all I saw was how Justin's presence in our lives had stressed and strained our marriage. Now I knew that sharing the difficult times we had in raising Justin had also deepened our commitment to each other and to our life together.

At home I allowed myself free rein of all my emotions. I felt the force of all these parental fears that Ruth Sullivan describes (Sullivan 1997). What is going on in the house where Justin lives? Will the staff know or care enough about what makes him happy? Will they know when his feet are cold at night? Who will touch him lovingly or rub his back at night? Will they make sure that he looks nice? How long will it be before Justin considers "home" the place that is not ours? Will he believe that we have abandoned him? Or will he believe that we don't love him anymore? How will we cope with the emptiness at home?

I worried about how Justin would adjust to this transition. While I had taken him to visit the home when we applied, I am sure moving in was quite a shock. Because of his cognitive limitations I could not prepare him for this move. One day, his world revolved around a home and a job where he was comfortable and familiar with the people and the routines. Then suddenly he was one of five other residents in a new house and a new farm where he didn't know the people or what was expected of him. I believe that at first he was depressed. He would not leave his room; he clung to his teddy bear and he slept a lot. He did not want to eat and he lost weight. His gastrointestinal problems and behavior issues flared up. It broke my heart to see him so unhappy. The staff reassured me that his reactions to this transition were normal. They convinced me that they were willing and prepared to do whatever it took to help Justin feel at home. Throughout all his difficult early days at the farm, I never felt that they did not want him there. Their commitment and compassion helped me hold on to the belief that he would eventually adjust.

I could empathize with Justin because I felt thrown out of my comfort zone as well. My biggest surprise was the initial disconnect I felt between my head and my heart. In my head, I was completely confident that this was the right time, right place, and right people for Justin's move to his new home. But in my heart I had the nagging feeling I had done something terribly wrong. So much of my life had been defined by activities and worries about Justin's care. Now I had given over my son and my job for the last 26 years to the care and keeping of somebody else.

I struggled to figure out my new role. After Justin moved to the farm, I knew he was having a difficult time managing his behavior. When I called and spoke to the staff, they would update me about his behavior with gentle honesty and assure me of their ability and willingness to help Justin adjust. Yet when I hung up the phone, I felt terrible. If Justin had a bad day when he lived at home, I could intervene and feel like I was doing what was needed to fix the situation. Doing something gave me a sense of control, even if it didn't always solve the problem. Now I hung up the phone and felt utterly powerless. Unsure of what to do next, I would sit down and engage in a mental tug-of-war. I wanted to stay involved and work with the staff to help Justin. (I also wanted them to think I was a good and involved parent.) Yet when I called, I could not fix the problems. I had not expected it would be so hard to continue to make these phone calls. What I wanted to do was not to call and to pretend that everything was just fine. Feeling powerless to help Justin's transition added to my grief.

Over the course of the next several months I tried to work through my grief. I allowed myself to take a deep breath, spend some time alone, and to just be where I was on any given day. I was more seasoned in how to deal with grief than I had been when Justin was first diagnosed. Over the intervening years I had gained more experience as I lost my parents and several close friends. By now I knew that there are no shortcuts through grief. I tried to avoid jumping back into my life and staying busy to bypass all the emotion I needed to face. Unlike the time when Justin was diagnosed, I knew this time would be painful, but necessary; uncomfortable, but not incapacitating. Most important, I knew it would not last forever.

It took Justin about six months to adjust to his move. He gradually engaged in life outside his bedroom by participating in activities and developing relationships with the staff. He became more active in the work of the farm, though the staff know that work is not his favorite part of the day. They have confirmed my observation that finding the right job to engage Justin's interests is not the issue. Justin's vocational interests rest primarily in *avoiding* work. (He has a "severely normal" side as well.) Luckily for him, he lives in an environment that is flexible, as a recent conversation illustrates. His social worker told me that the staff had given Justin a break from work to roller-skate on the driveway next to his house. But because the driveway is not very long, they thought he might get bored. So they let him create his own roller-skating rink by opening the front and back doors of his house and allowing him to skate through the house, out to the patio, and around to the driveway. I am not sure it gets more creative and flexible than that.

I started to feel better about Justin's move as I got to know the staff at his farm. When I stopped by to visit, they did not seem uncomfortable with letting me observe their interactions with Justin. They sought and incorporated my advice in how to meet his needs. They were responsive to my requests for information and my concerns. I saw evidence of a "checks and balances" system that identified and corrected problems when they occurred. It appeared to me that the staff really understood and enjoyed Justin. I am also fortunate to have long-standing relationships with many of the other Carolina Farms parents. It increases my confidence when other parents see the same good care that I do. It also gives me a committed group of parents who will work together to support the mission and the programs of the non-profit agency that runs the farm.

Other parents and professionals warned me that it would take at least a year for me to adjust to Justin's move, and it did. After a year, I began to feel that my heart and my head were finally catching up with each other. When Justin comes home now, he is happy to be here, but is not unhappy when it's time to go back. I find that I feel the same way. The two-hour drive back to the farm does not seem so far as it takes me through some beautiful North Carolina countryside. I am also fortunate to have Justin's former care providers available to provide some of his weekend transportation.

There are certain things I really enjoy about Justin's move to his new home. I love not recruiting, training, supervising, and paying for additional care providers. I love coordinating his care with one agency, and not five or six. I view Justin's sleeping problems when he comes home with a new equanimity. I know I will be able to get a full night of uninterrupted sleep when he goes back. I love not having a life where I am always multitasking. When he is home, about two weekends a month and on holiday vacations, I clear my calendar and focus totally on him. The rest of the time I am in control of my time and can plan my own schedule. I am now able to return to full-time work with the Autism Society of North Carolina. Having been so fortunate to find a quality program for Justin, I feel a passion and an obligation to help create similar opportunities for other families as well.

We are at a time in our family life when we are redefining all our family relationships. Michael is out of college and Patrick is not far behind. When they were young, Rob and I made it clear that we did not expect them to take Justin into their homes when they were older. We told them that we would find a great place for Justin to live with other people who would take good care of him. We wanted Michael and Patrick to pursue their own lives, but we hoped they would stay involved in Justin's as well. Now that they are adults, I believe there are new opportunities for them to have a different kind of relationship with Justin than was possible when they were young. It is time for our family to begin more specific conversations about what they would like their relationship with Justin to be. As this is new territory for all of us, I am not quite sure of the best way to proceed. Michael and Patrick are still too young to be Justin's guardians, but my hope is that they eventually will want to share that role. If they decide to accept the role of Justin's guardians, they will need support, preparation, and training along the way.

In the meantime, we have a guardian named in our will and any inheritance for Justin designated in a special needs trust. We also have written a letter of intent that accompanies our wills. It describes all the things we want in place to support a quality life for Justin when we are gone. It names an advisory committee of friends and professionals we have asked to stay involved in Justin's life and to help advise his guardian. Our aim is to keep Justin surrounded by people who will assure that he is getting the support and the care that he needs.

When Justin left home, I found that I had both the time and the need to write in my journal about the experience of being Justin's mother. Many of my stories in this book discuss the losses that I felt when Justin was first diagnosed. Perhaps it is fitting to end this chapter on letting go with a description of what I believe I have gained:

> So what have I gained from being Justin's parent? An extraordinary relationship with a high-maintenance, low-functioning, difficult young man with a killer smile, a mischievous sense of humor, and a charm all his own. The defining relationship of my life has brought me (literally and figuratively) kicking and screaming into a life I did not want, but now cannot imagine being without. If, as Judith Viorst tells us in *Necessary Losses*, our growth as human beings is inextricably linked to our losses, parenting Justin has forced me to grow into a better person than I believed myself to be (Viorst 1986, p.5). For how could I not learn to be courageous when I witnessed his courage in facing a world that so often scares and confuses him? How could I not learn forgiveness from a child who never held a grudge despite my parental failures? And how could I not learn about the difficult demands of love when living with someone who could sometimes act so unlovable? Surely it taught me that love is not just a feeling, but also a choice.
>
> I have had remarkable teachers throughout my life. Yet the most important lessons in my life over the last quarter century have come from (many would say) the least likely source – my son, Justin. In this future that I did not expect, I miss his presence in my daily life. My heaviest responsibility, he has also been my greatest gift.

Lessons we learned about letting go

1. Letting go is a process that we are still experiencing as Justin and Eric move into adulthood. As parents of adult children, letting go requires us to create new roles and relationships with our young adults and the professionals who work with them.

2. Our dreams for Justin and Eric are quite similar to our dreams for our typical children: that they will be safe, happy, fulfilled by work that is meaningful to them, and surrounded by people whom they care about and who care about them.

3. All times of transition require us to take risks that can make us feel a variety of uncomfortable emotions such as fear, sadness, and powerlessness. But we also experience pride and amazement at what Justin and Eric are learning and accomplishing as young adults.

4. Transition services are now a mandated service for young adults with autism. Become familiar with how your school approaches transition planning. Educate yourself about the services your young adult may need after leaving school by talking with other parents and professionals, visiting programs, and studying written information.

5. A good Transition Plan reflects you and your young adult's dreams and is based on a realistic assessment of your young adult's strengths, abilities, needs, and interests. Work on transition goals that will prepare your young adult to be as independent in self-care, self-advocacy, communication, and decision making as possible.

6. Having good services to support our children was a vital part of our letting Eric and Justin leave home. The entire autism community needs to work together to improve the quality and availability of services for all adults with autism and their families.

Student Information Sheet

Student's name: _____

Current teacher's name: _____

Subject, grade, or classroom: _____

1. What do you enjoy about this student?

2. What are some of the student's strengths, areas of progress, motivators, and interests?

3. What teaching strategies have been most effective with this student?

4. What strategies have not worked for you in the past?

5. What are this student's greatest challenges?

6. Do you have any behavioral strategies that you would like to share?

7. Who are some of the student's friends? Can they make the transition together?

8. Describe some of the ways in which the student participated in your class.

9. Please list any physical or health information (medications, sensory issues, motor abilities, etc.) that had to be accommodated in your class.

10. Other information you would like to share:

If there are additional questions, I can be reached at: _____

This has been adapted, with permission, from a document entitled *For the Teacher: Student Information Sheet* produced by Exceptional Children's Assistance Center (ECAC), 907 Barra Row, Suites 102/103, Davidson, NC 28036, tel: (704) 892-1321. www.ecac-parentcenter.org.

Books that Made a Difference

We had an opposite approach when it came to using books as a resource.

Ann

I read everything I could find about autism when Eric was first diagnosed. I needed to feel connected to someone who knew what my life was like, someone who shared my fears. I also needed to learn as much as I could about this complicated disorder that we were living with.

Maureen

I never read books about autism when Justin was first diagnosed. The personal stories gave me neither the reassurance nor the hope I desperately sought. I found comfort in books that offered insight or advice on how to live with our losses and move on with our lives.

The good news is that there is a wealth and diversity of resources in books that are available for parents today. What follows is an eclectic mix of autism and non-autism books that we found helpful over the years.

Asperger's Syndrome: A Guide for Parents and Professionals
by Tony Attwood (1998) Jessica Kingsley Publishers
This book provides parents and professionals with a basic overview of Asperger Syndrome (AS). The author incorporates case studies and frequently-asked questions into the text, and he covers such topics as diagnosis, social behavior, language, motor clumsiness, cognition, and sensory sensitivities.

Asperger's…What Does it Mean to Me? Structured Teaching Ideas for Home and School by Catherine Faherty (2000) Future Horizons
This manual is an in-depth resource designed to help children with AS and high-functioning autism (HFA) learn more about their diagnosis and themselves. Each chapter is divided into two parts: the first is a workbook containing pages for children to fill in, and the second is a section containing related ideas and practical strategies for parents and teachers.

Asperger Syndrome in the Family: Redefining Normal by Liane Holliday Willey (2001) Jessica Kingsley Publishers
In her first book, *Pretending to Be Normal*, the author described what it was like to grow up with AS. In this follow-up volume, the author discusses what it is like to be a wife and mother with AS (her youngest daughter also has AS).

The Autism Book: Answers to Your Most Pressing Questions by S. Jhoanna Robledo and Dawn Ham-Kucharski (2005) Penguin Group
Written specifically for parents and caregivers, this book contains over 100 questions and answers about autism spectrum disorder (ASD) in the following key areas: diagnosis, causes, manifestations, family emotions, treatments and interventions, family and relationship issues, parenting and lifestyle issues, the educational system, and ASD in adulthood.

Autism Spectrum Disorders: The Complete Guide to Understanding Autism, Asperger's Syndrome, Pervasive Developmental Disorder, and Other ASDs by Chantal Sicile-Kira (2004) The Berkley Publishing Group, Penguin Group
The author, a parent of a child with ASD and a former professional in the field, has spent years researching ASD. This reference guide was written to help parents, professionals, and other members of the community learn more about ASD, and it presents a thorough overview of the disorder, from diagnosis through adulthood.

Beyond the Wall: Personal Experiences with Autism and Asperger Syndrome by Stephen M. Shore (2001) Autism Asperger Publishing Co.
The author, who has AS, offers an autobiographical account of what it is like to live with the disorder.

Children with Autism: A Parent's Guide edited by Michael D. Powers (1989) Woodbine House
Considered a definitive reference, this book contains valuable information for both parents of newly-diagnosed children as well as experienced advocates. Chapter topics include ASD defined, diagnosis, medical problems and treatments, family life, education, advocacy, legal rights, and adults with ASD.

The Curious Incident of the Dog in the Nighttime by Mark Haddon (2003) Doubleday, Random House
This is a novel narrated by a 15-year-old teenager with HFA. The book gives the reader insight into the mind of a person on the autism spectrum.

A Difference in the Family: Living with a Disabled Child by Helen Featherstone (1980) Basic Books, Inc.
Drawing on interviews with parents and professionals, research, and her own personal experience, the author provides reassurance and invaluable guidance to families with a child with disabilities.

Elijah's Cup: A Family's Journey into the Community and Culture of High-Functioning Autism and Asperger's Syndrome by Valerie Paradiz (2005) Jessica Kingsley Publishers
This provocative and pioneering book is both a refreshing exploration of the history of ASDs and a powerful story of the author's own struggle with her son Elijah's AS.

Emergence: Labeled Autistic by Temple Grandin and Margaret M. Scariano (1986) Arena Press
A first-person portrayal of what it is like to experience autism spectrum disorder. The author, now a well-known scientist and speaker, recounts her memories as a child and young adult with ASD.

**Getting Past No: Negotiating Your Way From Confrontation
to Cooperation** by William Ury (1993) Bantam Books
A state-of-the-art book that outlines a practical five-step method for difficult negotiations with difficult people. Provides strategies for turning adversaries into negotiating partners.

Getting to Yes: Negotiating Agreement Without Giving In by
Roger Fisher, William Ury, and Bruce Patton (1991) Penguin Books
Highly readable, practical book that offers a concise step-by-step proven strategy for coming to mutually acceptable agreements in every sort of conflict.

Gift from the Sea by Anne Morrow Lindbergh (1955) Random
House, Inc.
With an inimitable combination of unselfconscious grace and transparent clarity, the author gives moving and memorable form to the problems that beset the human heart.

**How to Understand People Who Are Different: The
Combined Edition** by anonymous author (1994) Eladrel
Publishing House
An inside look at autism. The autistic author is 18 years old, mostly nonverbal, and communicates primarily through American Sign Language. However, he is very capable of expressing himself in print. He gives some straightforward explanations of how some people who are different experience life, along with helpful suggestions for how others might make that person feel more at ease with his or her surroundings.

Let Your Life Speak: Listening for the Voice of Vocation by
Parker J. Palmer (2000) John C. Wiley Books
With wisdom, compassion, and gentle humor, the author invites us to listen to our inner voice and follow its leadings to a sense of meaning and purpose.

**A Mind Apart: Understanding Children with Autism and
Asperger Syndrome** by Peter Szatmari, M.D. (2004) Guilford Press
Through moving stories of children he has worked with, the author helps us see the world through the eyes of a child with ASD. This com-

passionate book shows how gaining a better sense of your child's experience can deepen the bonds that support learning and growth.

Necessary Losses: The Loves, Illusions, Dependencies, and Impossible Expectations that All of Us Have to Give Up in Order to Grow by Judith Viorst (1986) Ballantine Books
A life-affirming and life-changing book on how we grow and change through the losses that are an inevitable and necessary part of life.

Parent Survival Manual: A Guide to Crisis Resolution in Autism and Related Developmental Disorders edited by Eric Schopler (1995) Plenum Press
This book is based on extensive research conducted by Division TEACCH. It contains 350 anecdotes contributed by parents that illustrate solutions to common behavior problems in children with ASD. After each anecdote is presented, an analysis of the parental intervention is provided.

A Parent's Guide to Asperger Syndrome and High-Functioning Autism: How to Meet the Challenges and Help Your Child Thrive by Sally Ozonoff, Geraldine Dawson, and James McPartland (2002) Guilford Press
This is a complete handbook for parents of children with AS and HFA. The authors clearly define these disorders, and they also offer detailed information on causes, diagnosis, and treatment.

Pretending to be Normal: Living with Asperger's Syndrome by Liane Holliday Willey (1999) Jessica Kingsley Publishers
The author, who has AS, has written this autobiography to illustrate what it is like to live with AS in different phases of life. The author describes her childhood and college years, including her social struggles and problems with sensory perception.

Quirky Kids: Understanding and Helping Your Child Who Doesn't Fit In – When to Worry and When Not to Worry by Perri Klass, M.D. and Eileen Costello, M.D. (2003) Ballantine Books
Written by two well-known pediatricians, this book focuses on children who do things differently and who may be diagnosed with a variety of

(and often overlapping) medical and psychiatric disorders. The authors wrote this guide to help parents navigate myriad assessments, diagnoses, therapies, and medications, and they offer help at every stage of a child's development.

Running with Walker: A Memoir by Robert Hughes (2003)
Jessica Kingsley Publishers
The author, a keen observer and gifted writer, presents an absorbing father's account of the first 15 years of Walker's life. He discusses in great detail Walker's development, the family's frustrating experiences with doctors and other professionals, and Walker's ongoing medical issues, ranging from sleep problems to seizures.

Siblings of Children with Autism: A Guide for Families by
Sandra L. Harris and Beth A. Glasberg (2003) Woodbine House, Inc.
An in-depth look at what it is like to grow up as a sibling of a child with autism. The authors offer practical, down-to-earth advice grounded in sound research and aided by the wisdom of their clinical work with siblings.

The Siege: The First Eight Years of an Autistic Child by Clara
Claiborne Park (1967) Little, Brown and Company
This illuminating memoir is one of the first personal accounts of ASD, and it is now regarded as a classic. It is a mother's story of raising a daughter with ASD at a time when the medical community knew little about the disorder and its treatment.

A Slant of Sun: One Child's Courage by Beth Kephart (1998)
Quill/William Morrow and Company, Inc.
This beautifully written memoir tells the author's story of life with her son, Jeremy, who was diagnosed with pervasive developmental disorder–not otherwise specified in 1991. This is a moving, intimate story of love, courage, and hope.

Succeeding in College with Asperger Syndrome: A Student Guide by John Harpur, Maria Lawlor, and Michael Fitzgerald (2004) Jessica Kingsley Publishers
A book written to help students with AS meet the challenges of college life. This is a comprehensive handbook that addresses a wide range of important and complex issues, ranging from academics to interactions with the opposite sex.

Tasks Galore by Laurie Eckenrode, Pat Fennell, and Kathy Hearsey (2003) Self-published
Written by teachers and therapists who are highly experienced in Structured Teaching methodology, this book offers a compilation of 250 tasks shown in color photographs. These tasks provide numerous ideas to spark creativity of parents, teachers, and therapists as they individualize a program for their students. There are two additional books in the series: *Tasks Galore for the Real World* and *Tasks Galore: Making Groups Meaningful.*

Traveling Mercies: Some Thoughts on Faith by Anne Lamott (1999) Pantheon Books
A chronicle of faith and spirituality that is at once tough, personal, affectionate, wise, and very funny.

When Bad Things Happen to Good People by Harold S. Kushner (1981) Avon Books
A compassionate and deeply moving book that brings us renewed faith, comfort, and inspiration.

References

American Academy of Pediatrics, Committee on Children with Disabilities (2001) "The Pediatrician's Role in the Diagnosis and Management of Autistic Spectrum Disorder in Children." Available on http://pediatrics.aappublications.org/ cgi/content/full/107/5/e85.

Baldwin, J. (1998) *Collected Essays*. New York: Library of America.

Ballance, E. (2005) "How to Relax and Relieve Stress." Presentation given at the Autism Society of North Carolina Annual Conference, April 8.

Bartlett, J. (1992) *Bartlett's Familiar Quotations*. Boston: Little, Brown and Company.

Bristol-Power, M. (2000) "Research in Autism: New Directions." *The Advocate*, July–August, 16–17.

Buechner, F. (1977) *Telling the Truth: The Gospel as Tragedy, Comedy and Fairy Tale*. San Francisco: Harper San Francisco.

Cameron, J. (1998) *The Right to Write: An Invitation and Initiation into the Writing Life*. New York: Jeremy P. Tarcher/Putnam, Penguin Putnam, Inc.

Centers for Disease Control and Prevention, National Center on Birth Defects and Developmental Disabilities (2005) Available on www.cdc.gov/ncbddd/dd/aix/ about/default.htm.

Covey, S. (1997) *The Seven Habits of Highly Effective Families*. New York: Golden Books Publishing Co., Inc.

Debbaudt, D. (2002) *Autism, Advocates, and Law Enforcement Professionals: Recognizing and Reducing Risk Situations for People with Autism Spectrum Disorders*. London: Jessica Kingsley Publishers.

Featherstone, H. (1980) *A Difference in the Family: Living with a Disabled Child*. New York: Basic Books, Inc.

Fielding, H. (2003) *Olivia Joules and the Overactive Imagination*. New York: Penguin Books.

Fisher, R., Ury, W. and Patton, B. (1991) *Getting to Yes: Negotiating Agreement Without Giving In*. 2nd edition. New York: Penguin Books.

Goodman, E. and O'Brien, P. (2000) *I Know Just What You Mean: The Power of Friendship in Women's Lives*. New York: Fireside, Simon & Schuster.

Guthrie Medlen, J. (2004) "Everything Will Change." *Disability Solutions,* September–October, 2.

Harmon, A. (2004) "How About Not 'Curing' Us, Some Autistics are Pleading." *The New York Times,* December 20, p.A1.

Harris, S. and Glasberg, B. (2003) *Siblings of Children with Autism: A Guide for Families.* 2nd edition. Bethesda, MD: Woodbine House, Inc.

Hax, C. (2005) "Tell Me About It." *Raleigh News and Observer,* August 10, 6E.

Holliday Willey, L. (1999) *Pretending to be Normal: Living with Asperger's Syndrome.* London: Jessica Kingsley Publishers.

Kierkegaard, S. (1948) *Purity of Heart is to Will One Thing.* New York: Harper and Row.

Kushner, H.S. (2003) *The Lord is My Shepherd: Healing Wisdom of the Twenty-Third Psalm.* New York: Alfred A. Knopf.

Lamott, A. (2005) *Plan B: Further Thoughts on Faith.* New York: Riverhead, Penguin Group, Inc.

Lindbergh, A.M. (1955) *Gift from the Sea.* New York: Random House, Inc.

Norris, K. (1997) *The Psalms: With Commentary by Kathleen Norris.* Riverhead Sacred Text Series. New York: The Berkley Publishing Group.

Page, R. (1980) "Workers Who Have Autism: What You Need to Know – What You Need to Forget." Paper given at the International Symposium on Hard to Train Youth, Dearborn, Michigan.

Palmer, A. (2006) *Realizing the College Dream with Autism or Asperger Syndrome: A Parent's Guide to Student Success.* London: Jessica Kingsley Publishers.

Quindlen, A. (2005) "The Good Enough Mother." *Newsweek,* February 21, 50–1.

Roosevelt, E. (1960) *You Learn by Living.* New York: Harper and Brothers Publishers, Inc.

Spicer, D. (2005) "Closing Keynote." Presentation given at the Autism Society of North Carolina Annual Conference, April 9.

Stout, H. (2004) "The Key to a Lasting Marriage: Combat." *Wall Street Journal,* November 4, D8.

Sullivan, R. (1997) "When Your Son/Daughter Leaves Home: Heartbreak? Relief? Or Both?" *Newsletter of the Autism Services Center,* Winter, 2.

Ury, W. (1993) *Getting Past No: Negotiating Your Way From Confrontation to Cooperation.* New York: Bantam Books.

Viorst, J. (1986) *Necessary Losses: The Loves, Illusions, Dependencies, and Impossible Expectations that All of Us Have to Give Up in Order to Grow.* New York: Ballantine Books.